**Sports Illustrated**

# FULL THROTTLE

## FROM DAYTONA TO DARLINGTON

PHOTOGRAPH BY TOM WHITMORE/ICON SMI

# FULL
# THROTTLE
## FROM DAYTONA TO DARLINGTON

**Sports Illustrated**

POCONO 500, JUNE 8, 2003

PHOTOGRAPH BY JAMIE SQUIRE/GETTY IMAGES

# CONTENTS

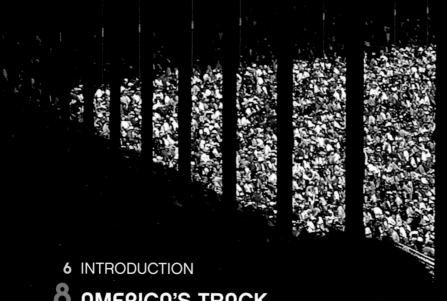
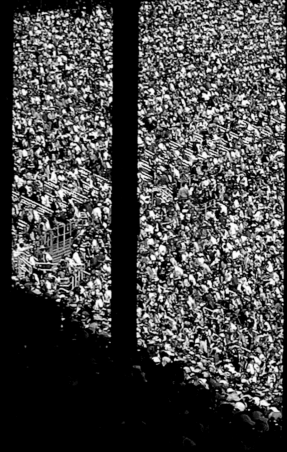

**SPORTS ILLUSTRATED**
**Managing Editor** Terry McDonell **President** E. Bruce Hallett

**Editor** Sandy Bailey
**Art Director** Craig Gartner
**Senior Editors** Richard O'Brien, Bobby Clay
**Photo Editor** Jeffrey Weig
**Chief of Reporters** Trisha Blackmar
**Associate Editor** David Sabino (statistics)
**Staff Writers** Mark Bechtel, Stephen Cannella
**Special Contributor** Jeff MacGregor
**Writer-Reporters** Lars Anderson, Richard Deitsch
**Reporters** Lisa Altobelli, Mark Beech,
Pete McEntegart, Julia Morrill, Andrea Woo
**Assistant Art Director** Melissa Devlin
**Assistant Photo Editor** Kari Stein
**Copy Editors** Kevin Kerr, Nancy Ramsey,
Rich Donnelly, Denis Johnston
**Editorial Assistant** Bryan Byers
**Director, New Product Development** Bruce Kaufman

**TIME INC. HOME ENTERTAINMENT**
**President** Rob Gursha
**Vice President, Branded Businesses** David Arfine
**Executive Director, Marketing Services** Carol Pittard
**Director, Retail and Special Sales** Tom Mifsud
**Director of Finance** Tricia Griffin
**Assistant Marketing Director** Niki Whelan
**Prepress Manager** Emily Rabin
**Marketing Manager** Michelle Kuhr
**Associate Book Production Manager** Suzanne Janso

**OUT OF THE SHADOWS**
CARS FLY PAST THE
TEXAS MOTOR SPEEDWAY
GRANDSTAND DURING THE
2003 SAMSUNG/RADIO SHACK
500 OUTSIDE FORT WORTH.

**PHOTOGRAPH BY
JONATHAN FERREY/GETTY IMAGES**

COPYRIGHT 2004
TIME INC. HOME ENTERTAINMENT

PUBLISHED BY SPORTS ILLUSTRATED BOOKS

TIME INC.
1271 AVENUE OF THE AMERICAS
NEW YORK, N.Y. 10020

SPORTS ILLUSTRATED BOOKS IS A TRADEMARK OF TIME INC.

ISBN: 1-932273-17-4
LIBRARY OF CONGRESS CONTROL NUMBER: 2003097876

THIS BOOK WAS PUBLISHED WITHOUT THE AUTHORIZATION OF NASCAR. NASCAR IS A REGISTERED
TRADEMARK OF THE NATIONAL ASSOCIATION FOR STOCK CAR AUTORACING, INC.

# INTRODUCTION by Jeff MacGregor

STRANGELY, there is grace in it. Coming down out of that fourth turn at Daytona hard on the gas to the green flag, 43 cars begin their season running two by two and wheel to wheel and nose to tail in a line as lithe and supple as a wave. And when that wave breaks across the frontstretch, pouring color and power and noise over the grandstands, a quarter of a million fans rise to their feet screaming, and the sound of those engines and those people rumbles up from the center of the earth and comes down at you, and the sound is everywhere, deafening and electric, scattering your thoughts like birds,

**SCENES FROM A SEASON** THOUGH (FROM LEFT) MATT KENSETH REIGNED, '03 ALSO BELONGED TO ROBBY GORDON'S PIT CREW, CARS SPINNING AT RICHMOND, DAYTONA'S FAB FANS, JEFF GORDON AT MARTINSVILLE AND THE TALLADEGA INFIELD FAITHFUL.

until the only thing left is pure sensation, and the only thing you see or hear is that long line of cars speeding past you fluid and alive. It is the sound of it you love first, and the sound of it never changes.

A turning world insists on change, though, and the 2004 NASCAR season brings with it more changes than the sport has seen in two generations—new sponsorships, new manufacturers, new fans, new faces and names and places and dates. Everything will be different this year. A new wave. But everything will be the same.

The drivers will still be stock car drivers. That their names are Kenseth or Newman or Johnson, McMurray or Stewart or

Busch, changes nothing. Young as they are, they'll still bump and run, still take the air off each other's rear decks, still rub and bang and beat their way through the field. They'll run each other up the track at Thunder Valley and run each other down in the first turn at Thunder Road. They'll run the high groove at Darlington and run low and fast and four wide at Talladega. They'll win races and lose championships by the width of a battered fender, by the length of a single heartbeat.

Pearson and Yarborough and Isaac are gone, and Baker and Byron and Flock, but there are still Wallaces to run against, after

Pearson and Yarborough and Isaac are gone, but there are still Wallaces to run against, and Labontes, Burtons and Bodines. And another Earnhardt. **This one on the brink, perhaps, of his own greatness.**

all, and Labontes, Burtons and Bodines. There's Martin and Rudd and Elliott, too; and a Waltrip and a Jarrett and a Petty. And another Earnhardt. This one on the brink, perhaps, of his own greatness. And the changing young faces of racing will still chase Jeff Gordon, ancient four-time champion and alltime money winner, now 32 years old.

The crews will still stand at the gate outside the garages at 6:55 a.m. waiting for a drowsy security guard to let them in at seven. After a 40-hour week at the shop, they'll put in another 40 hours at the track. Still, they won't expect anyone who doesn't already know them to remember their names.

Millions of fans will still arrive on Mondays for the next Sunday's race, camping the hillsides at Bristol and the sandy flats at Dover and that little holler beyond the railroad tracks at Martinsville. They will eat too much and drink too much and play Kid Rock and Skynyrd much too loudly. They'll keep waiting by the fence for a driver's autograph. They'll keep yelling, "Drive it like you stole it!" when they get one. They will keep coming back, every year, more and more of them, because love is patient with change.

The cars are still just cars, of course, as beautiful and useless as jewels, as low and wide and powerful as appetite itself.

And week in and week out those cars and those drivers will come down out of that fourth turn at Daytona, or at Fontana or Atlanta or Richmond, hard on the gas to the checkered flag, in a line as long and graceful as a river, a river running fast and deep all the way back into time. And the sound of it all, that unmistakable music of a big V-8 running wide open, running hard for money and glory and love, won't ever change. Unchanged, it is the sound of America, ever-changing. □

# AMERICA

Much more than just a nice place to watch a race, Daytona has always been synonymous with fun in the sun, speed—and some of the greatest moments in the history of NASCAR

PHOTOGRAPH BY DAVID WALBERG

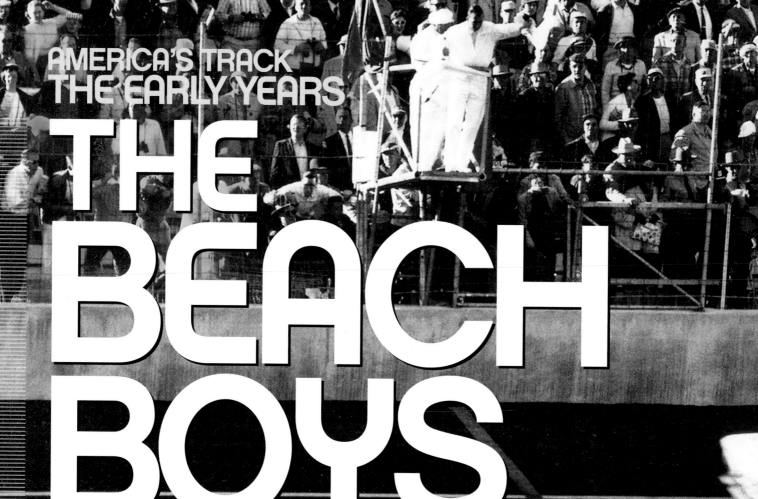

# AMERICA'S TRACK
# THE EARLY YEARS
# THE BEACH BOYS

The unveiling of Big Bill France's colossal new track in February 1959 brought speed lovers and speed records back to Daytona Beach

## by Kenneth Rudeen

**FIRST FINISH** LEE PETTY (42) WON THE 500 IN '59 BY EDGING OUT JOHNNY BEAUCHAMP (73). JOE WEATHERLY (48) WAS A LAP DOWN.

DAYTONA BEACH has been up to its sunburned neck in automotive speed since the early 1900s. In the get-a-horse days romantic daredevils like Barney Oldfield furrowed the smooth sands at the Atlantic's edge, and for a time world-famous seekers of absolute land-speed records brought their monsters to the same inviting shore. But since the mid-1930s, when the speed-record men changed

allegiance to the vast Bonneville Salt Flats of Utah, Daytona has not been able to boast the superlative *fastest*.

All that is now changed by the fact that Daytona has a magnificent new automobile racetrack, and if it is not the fastest in the world, a lot of citizens will have to eat their hats.

This impressive racing plant is called Daytona International Speedway. It is the greatest achievement of a rumpled, 49-year-old, deceptively casual giant of a man named William Henry Getty France. Many other hands were involved in it, to be sure, but it was Bill France who dreamed the dream and bulldozed it through.

Six years in the planning and more than a year building, the speedway sprawls over what was a swampy pine-and-cypress thicket on the western edge of Daytona. The city airport is conveniently near, as is a one-fifth-mile dog-racing track. A jai alai fronton is going up across the highway.

The principal element of the speedway is a 2½-mile superfast track of asphaltic concrete, banked at a steep 31 degrees in the two big turns and at 18 degrees in the apex of the fast dogleg past the grandstands. To the eye the high banks seem even steeper than 31 degrees; this illusion invariably draws oohs and aahs from visitors, and France gleefully says the view from the top is "like looking down off a jailhouse roof."

The lap distance of 2½ miles was candidly chosen to

## Weary of his dependence on the fickle sea, France had decided **Speed Week needed a reliable location.**

The 44-acre lake in the infield, nine feet at its deepest and 1,000 yards long, was made simply by digging down below the level of the water table. Part of the dirt removed was used to bulwark the banked sections of the track. (Everything but the squeal of the racers' tires, by the way, seems destined to be utilized in this project.) The lake—named for Daytona civic leader J. Saxton Lloyd, who worked assiduously to promote the speedway plan—will serve not only as an ornament but also as a site for hydroplane racing. Eventually there will be a football field on the plot of ground between the pit access road and the central grandstand.

equal that of the Indianapolis 500, this nation's foremost and the world's richest race, but the shape of the Daytona course is unique. It was conceived by France to make possible an unobstructed view from the grandstands. No part of the tri-oval track is obscured, nor does a spectator have to lean forward, past adjacent fans, to focus on distant action on the homestretch.

Already in place are grandstands seating 18,800 and portable bleachers accommodating 6,500 more. There is parking space for 35,000 cars in areas outside and in, and space in the enormous infield for approximately 75,000 spectators.

A road course of slightly more than two miles has been laid out in the infield. This will be used in conjunction with the speed track for road racing, providing a total lap distance of about 4½ miles. Additionally, there is a 3.56-mile course for motorcycle racing.

Every responsible racing official is acutely concerned with safety these days, and the solutions at Daytona seem to have been well thought out. A thick, steel-reinforced, 42-inch-high concrete wall extends along the outside of the track in front of the stands, which are well above track level. Above the wall is a 10-foot-high steel-mesh fence, and surmounting this is a mesh overhang, extending trackward, that is meant to trap any object that might fly off a racing car—a wheel, for example. A steel guardrail encloses the rest of the track.

Considered as a whole, the speedway is undoubtedly one of the very finest in the world. It is the only one to be built in the U.S. on what might be called a heroic scale since the Indianapolis Motor Speedway opened, in 1909. Many racecourses have been built in the U.S. in the last few years, and some are elaborate, but they are pri-

marily road, not track, courses, and none is so imposing as the Daytona operation. Only two other tracks stand comparison with it—the high-banked, 2.64-mile oval at Monza, Italy, and, of course, Indianapolis. The fastest track in the world today is the one at Monza, where the record average speed for a race is just more than 166 mph.

Stock cars tuning up for the three days of racing that climax the annual Daytona Speed Week have already bettered 143 mph on the new track. This is sensationally fast for stock cars—a speed equal to that of a very quick lap at the Brickyard by the far more powerful, much lighter roadsters.

When the Indianapolis cars make their first

**SPEED VISION**

BUILDING A TRACK ON THE RACE-RUTTED DUNES OF DAYTONA BEACH WAS A DREAM COME TRUE FOR FRANCE (TOP, ON LEFT, WITH LLOYD), WHO HOPED TO BUILD A SUPERSPEEDWAY THAT WOULD BECOME ONE OF THE FINEST IN THE WORLD.

visit to Daytona—in a 100-mile race on April 4, 1959—they are likely to reach speeds never before recorded by racing cars on a closed circuit. Lap speeds of 175 to 180 mph have been predicted by Thomas W. Binford ("a conservative estimate," he says), president of the U.S. Auto Club, which supervises racing in the Indianapolis 500.

There will undoubtedly be considerable gloating in Daytona when this occurs, because the citizenry is eager to see Indianapolis outdone, and the record for a single lap at the Brickyard is exactly 148.148 mph. Sheer speed alone, however, does not make a classic race. By its nature the Indianapolis track, fast as it is, could never yield the speeds expected at Daytona. Yet the 500 has been thriving for years, and it annually attracts one of the world's largest sports gatherings. It exudes tradition. And if it has no spectacularly steep turns, it does have four immensely difficult corners, which demand driving of a high order. Daytona will complement Indianapolis, then, not overshadow it, no matter how fast the new track proves to be or how astutely it is managed.

Indeed, France was aware when he began to consider designs that the track would have to outdo not Indianapolis but his own past promotions of the picturesque old beach-road course at Daytona. Weary of his dependence on the fickle sea for a raceworthy beach, he had decided years ago that the racing events of Speed Week must eventually be moved to a reliable location.

That he then set out to build a supertrack is characteristic of him. There are three things to keep in mind concerning Bill France: his doggedness; his flair for the dramatic; and his extraordinary ability to charm, win the confidence of and get constructive help from perfect strangers.

Here is an example. When already past the point of no return on the building of the dream track, Bill France Racing Inc., which France heads, still needed large financial commitments to be sure of the track's completion. One day France attended an airpower demonstration at Eglin (Fla.) Air Force Base, where he met Clint Murchison Jr., son of the gas-and-oil magnate from Texas. Young Murchison needed to make a quick trip to Miami, and France happened to have his private plane at hand. Result: An executive from Murchison's construction firm visited Daytona. Upon his recommendation, France obtained a $500,000 construction loan.

France has been turning on the charm ever since he arrived in Daytona in 1934, an automobile mechanic with a taste for racing.

"I'd always liked to fool around with race cars," he says. "I'd driven them some, and I'd gotten to love the smell of castor oil [once a popular lubricant]."

When Sir Malcolm Campbell, the last of the great Daytona speed merchants, forsook the beach for Bonneville in 1936, first the city and then the Elks Club promoted races at Daytona. These lost money. In '38 France, who had driven in these races, began to share in the management of subsequent events. When racing was resumed after World War II, he became the principal sponsor. Influential friends flocked to his side. Ultimately the stock car races on the 4.1-mile beach-road course and the passenger-car runs on the beach—the main ingredients of Speed Week—won national prominence.

Daytona has, year after year, crowded more and more events into Speed Week, and in honor of the opening of the track, the calendar is jammed as never before. But despite the practicing, qualifying, tire testing and traditional straightaway trials on the broad, flat sands beside the sea, what everyone is really waiting for is the onset of racing at the speedway. This will begin in earnest with a 100-mile dash for the NASCAR Grand National cars (late-model closed cars), to be followed by a 100-mile race for convertibles. Then the modified and sportsman cars, those jalopies with the wonderfully tuned engines, will have a 200-mile go. Finally, 64 closed cars and convertibles will slam into the first turn of the speedway in the featured event, a 500-mile race for the largest purse ever offered in stock car racing, $60,160.

"Over on the beach," France says, "the good Lord always looked after us. When things looked bad and we needed an east wind to send those big waves to smooth out the sand, we always got one just in time. If we keep getting the breaks, this track will have to be equal to any."

## 1979

# A FIST-PUMPING AFFAIR

*As a record number of people watched on television, Cale Yarborough (right) and Donnie Allison (left) made contact and hit the wall on the last lap of the Daytona 500, disabling both cars. Yarborough quickly got out and approached Donnie's brother Bobby (middle), who had stopped at the wreck site, and hit Bobby with his helmet, sparking a melee that is now known simply as the Fight.*

**PHOTOGRAPH BY RIC FELD/AP**

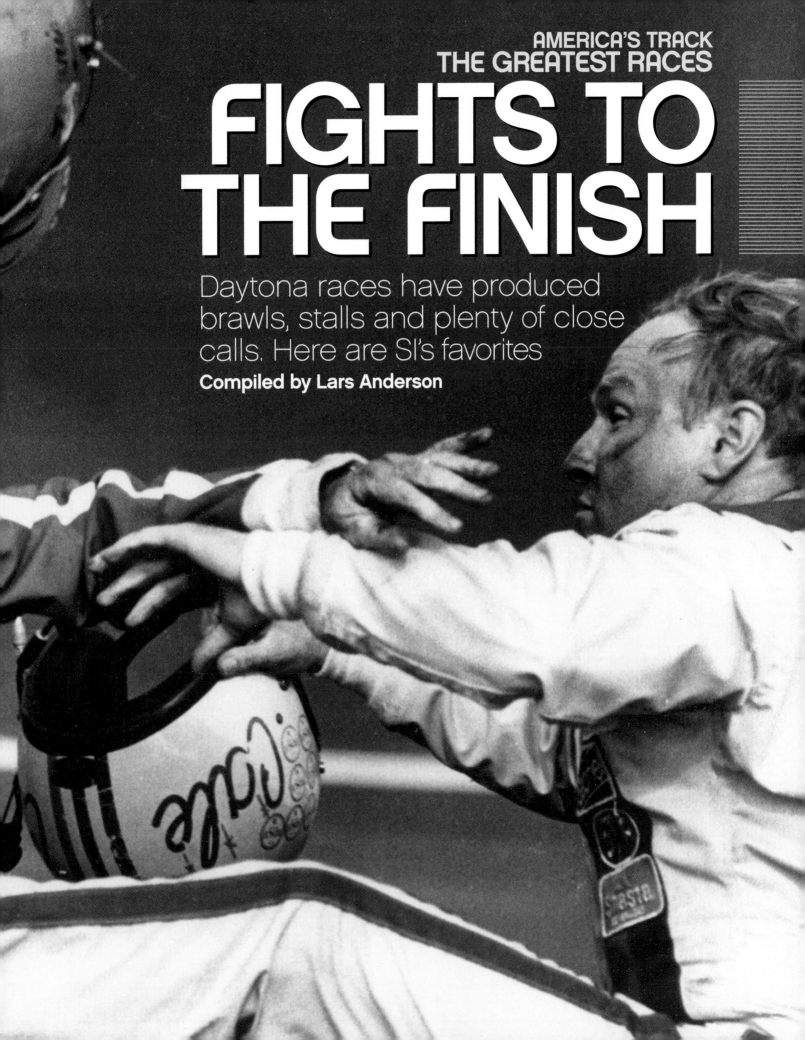

# FIGHTS TO THE FINISH

Daytona races have produced
brawls, stalls and plenty of close
calls. Here are SI's favorites

**Compiled by Lars Anderson**

# AN ENDING FOR THE AGES

*Two legends went flying down the backstretch on the final lap, exchanging the lead three times. First one, then the other hit the wall, and finally David Pearson (far right) limped past Richard Petty (below) and crossed the finish line at 10 mph. The drivers had finished one-two 57 times in the previous 13 years, but no race was more thrilling than this Daytona 500.*

**PHOTOGRAPH BY CORBIS**

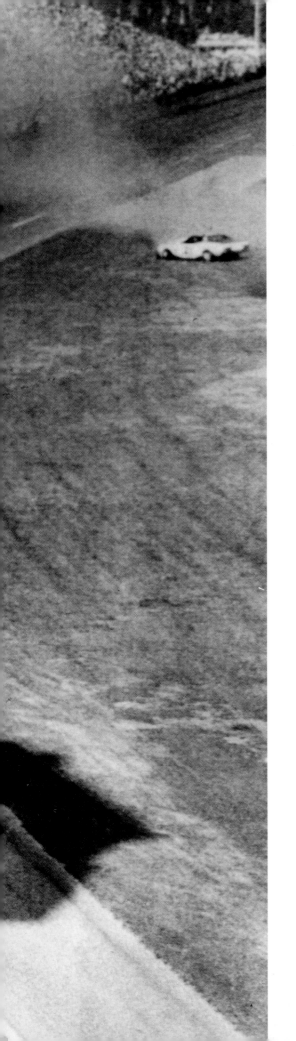

## 1964

### THE KING IS BORN

*This year was a special one for Richard Petty. Not only did he race to his first Daytona 500 victory on Feb. 23 in his signature number 43 Chevy, but he also went on to win the first of his seven point championships. His on-track success inspired legions of devoted fans, and he received the first of his nine most popular driver awards that season.*

**PHOTOGRAPH BY PETER CUSTER**

## 1977

### A CALE-FORCE VICTORY

*Amid swirling 30-mph winds, Cale Yarborough won his second Daytona 500, outracing Benny Parsons to the checkered flag. Known as NASCAR's original daredevil—as a child Yarborough caught water moccasins for fun, and he once wrestled an alligator—he would go on to win his second of three straight championships in '77.*

**PHOTOGRAPH BY ERIC SCHWEIKARDT**

## 1985

### AWESOME BILL

*Never before had one man so dominated Daytona. Bill Elliott earned the pole with a speed of 205.114 mph (at the time the fastest stock car lap ever), won his 125-mile qualifying race by two miles and then won the 500, which he celebrated in Victory Lane with his daughter Starr.*

**PHOTOGRAPH BY JOHN IACONO**

## 1998

### AT LAST . . . A BREAKTHROUGH

*Nineteen times Dale Earnhardt had tried to win the Daytona 500, and 19 times he'd failed. That made this day even more special, and everyone on pit road recognized this long overdue victory. "I've got that goddam monkey off my back," Earnhardt yelled in Victory Lane.*

**PHOTOGRAPH BY JIM GUND**

## GENERATION NEXT

**20 01**

*Five months after his father was killed on the last lap of the Daytona 500, Dale Earnhardt Jr. (in 13th position) returned for the Pepsi 400—and dominated just like his father used to. Junior led 108 of the first 145 laps and took the checkered flag. When he got out of his car, he didn't consider the past; all that mattered was the sweetness of the present. "It doesn't get any better than this," he said.*

**PHOTOGRAPH BY BOB ROSATO**

# 2004
## SEASON PREVIEW

We're goin' green! Over the next 20 pages you'll find all the stats you need to get ready for the Nextel Cup —plus the inside scoop on all 36 races from Darrell Waltrip

**PHOTOGRAPH BY JOHN BIEVER**

**THICK AS A BRICK**
THE TRAFFIC AT INDY, AS
AT EVERY RACE IN THE
NEW SEASON, WILL BE
BUMPER-TO-BUMPER,
WITH ABSOLUTELY
*NO* DELAYS

# GENERATION NEXTEL

A new sponsor, a new leader and a new schedule give good 'ol NASCAR a very different look for 2004
## by Mark Bechtel

IN JANUARY 2003 NASCAR introduced to the world "Realignment 2004 and Beyond"—which, it turns out, is a corporate marketing plan, not the worst *Star Trek* movie ever made. Instead of boldly going where no man had gone before, NASCAR boldly decided to no longer go where it had previously gone all the time. Which is to say, NASCAR moved its most tradition-steeped race, the Southern 500, from Labor Day to mid-November, in the process relocating it from Darlington, S.C., to California Speedway, the decidedly un-Southern track an hour east of Los Angeles.

There was a certain irony to changing the date of the Southern 500. Darlington was the South's first paved speedway and, as such, ushered stock car racing into a more modern era. "Without Darlington we'd still be racing on half-mile dirt tracks on Saturday night," says

Richard Petty. But even as newer, bigger, more fan-friendly tracks sprung up, Darlington remained largely unchanged, and the progress it helped create eventually rendered the Lady in Black outdated.

Drivers at the 2003 Southern 500 tended to guard their words when asked about the schedule shuffling, but nearly all acknowledged that they were saying goodbye to a special event. Said Ricky Craven, who hails from Newburgh, Maine, "I take my family to Fenway Park every year. It's part of being a New England boy. The last couple of years I've come into Darlington, I've had the same appreciation as I have when I walk down Yawkey Way, looking at the Green Monster. It has that presence, and it has that history." Fans were less tactful. There were several signs reading CALIFORNIA SUCKS and several more echoing the sentiment.

That backlash underscored NASCAR's challenge for 2004 and beyond: How does a sport that thrives on its blue-collar roots and embraces its history as tightly as it does become more mainstream without alienating its fan base? "This is just another step in modernizing tradition," NASCAR president Mike Helton said of moving the Labor Day race. "It's not forsaking it. Like we've said all along, we still maintain for our own benefit that tradition is important, but we still have to be conscious and responsible in growing the sport."

**RING IN THE NEW**
JEFF GORDON (MIDDLE) AND DALE EARNHARDT JR. (RIGHT) JOINED NEXTEL CEO TIM DONAHUE IN JUNE TO ANNOUNCE THE DEAL.

**PHOTOGRAPH BY RICHARD DREW/AP**

23

In each of its first 55 years NASCAR aged. In 2003 it grew up. It left the year way hipper, savvier and richer than it entered it. In a year in which the hottest TV show featured five gay men revamping the lifestyles of macho men, it was only fitting that NASCAR received the biggest, and unlikeliest, makeover of its life.

How NASCAR will look different in 2004:

• Its name. Last March, Winston, which has been the primary sponsor for NASCAR's top series since 1971, announced its desire to pull out of the sport. There had always been a certain good ol' boy synchronicity in the marriage. Racing and cigarettes go together like baseball and chaw, like poker and stogies. (Anyone who doubts this need only recall that until a few years ago smoking in the

**MOVIN'** THE LABOR DAY WEEKEND DARLINGTON STOP (BELOW AND OPPOSITE PAGE) WAS A CASUALTY OF NASCAR'S DESIRE TO EXPAND ON ITS SOUTHERN ROOTS.

pits was not only legal but also seemingly encouraged, the gallons of gasoline within the range of a flicked butt be damned.) But the restrictions placed on tobacco advertising made it too difficult for Winston to stay in the sport, so with four years remaining on a deal signed in 2002 it left. Rumored successors included McDonald's, Coca-Cola and Visa—established companies with broad appeal to NASCAR's traditional demographic—but after 100 days of pondering its future, NASCAR settled on Nextel, a telecommunications company. For NASCAR it was about as far away from its previous sponsor as it could get. The American tobacco industry has been around for the better part of four centuries; Nextel, which signed a 10-year deal with NASCAR worth $700 million, has barely been around 10 years.

Compared with Winston, though, Nextel brings so many more marketing opportunities to the table. Winston offered free smokes at the track. Nextel offers everything from the potential for real-time updates sent straight to a phone to phones that look like cars. "We've come a long way toward making NASCAR racing a national sport, with fans spread across America," NASCAR chairman Bill France

Jr. said when making the announcement. "We still have miles to go to achieve our goals, but we are confident we are well on our way."

• Its cars. While the common template continued to blur the lines between makes, the most significant development of the year was Toyota's announcement last February that it will compete in the Craftsman Truck Series this year, with an eye toward rolling out Cup cars by 2007—this despite the fact that the NASCAR rule book states that the sport is open to "American made" cars only. (The Toyota Tundra is made entirely within the United States.)

Predictably, some hard-core fans disapproved. "NASCAR is the last purely American sport," said a disgusted Carl Dover, 46, at the Winston. "The [Japanese] are into everything. I hope their engines blow up in every race." Meanwhile, Pontiac, which won the Winston Cup in 2000 and '02, announced in October it was leaving NASCAR in '04.

• Drivers. You want good ol' boys? You're going to have to look elsewhere. How much has the face of NASCAR changed in the past five years? Well, of the top seven drivers in last year's standings only two were driving Cup cars in 1998: Jeff Gordon and Matt Kenseth, who ran only one race. Throw in Kurt Busch, who finished 11th in the 2003 standings but won four races, and the eight drivers with the best chance to win the '04 championship—Ryan Newman, Gordon, Dale Earnhardt Jr., Jimmie Johnson, Busch, Kenseth, Kevin Harvick and Tony Stewart—are all 32 or younger.

And don't let the fact that Kenseth ran away with the 2003 points race fool you. Four drivers had more points than he did over the second half of the season.

• Leadership. In October, Bill France Jr., whose father founded NASCAR in a smoke-filled hotel bar in late 1947, announced he was stepping down as CEO and chairman of the board. He handed those titles to his

In each of its first 55 years NASCAR aged. In 2003 it grew up. **It left the year hipper, savvier and richer than it entered it.**

son, Brian, while his daughter, Lesa France Kennedy, a graduate of Duke, will run International Speedway Corporation, which controls the family's 13 tracks.

At the Realignment announcement in January, Bill showed that his old school, street-learned ways still had a place in the sport. When Brian's presentation got bogged down in buzzwords, Bill grabbed a microphone and spelled it out in layman's terms: Certain tracks weren't cutting it in terms of ticket sales, and they were going to lose races. End of discussion. In the end, though, the 70-year-old, who has had numerous health problems in recent years, realized that the sport's future was going to rest in the hands of a new generation, so he stepped down. "I had my fling at it, and now it's time, I think, to pass the mail," he said. "Life and time move on."

True. But some years they move a little faster than others.  □

# February

 Race 1

**DAYTONA 500**
**FEBRUARY 15, 2004** NETWORK: **NBC**
DAYTONA INTERNATIONAL SPEEDWAY
DAYTONA BEACH, FLA.
WWW.DAYTONAINTLSPEEDWAY.COM

**2003 WINNER:** Michael Waltrip
**FIRST RACE:** Feb. 22, 1959
**WINNER:** Lee Petty
**QUALIFYING RECORD:** Bill Elliott
210.364 mph, Feb. 9, 1987
**RACE RECORD:** Buddy Baker
177.602 mph, Feb. 17, 1980
**MOST WINS:** 7, Richard Petty
**TRACK SPECS:** 2.5-mile tri-oval, Turns 1–4
banked 31 degrees, tri-oval banked
18 degrees
**TRACK FACT:** It took three days of
examining finish line photos and newsreel
footage to declare Lee Petty the winner of the
first Daytona 500.

**DARRELL WALTRIP SAYS:** *The first
race of the year gives you an idea of
which teams are ready to battle for
the title. One question will be on
everybody's mind: Can anyone beat
Michael or Dale Jr.? The DEI guys
have won nine of the last 11
restrictor-plate races.*

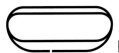 Race 2

**SUBWAY 400**
**FEBRUARY 22, 2004** NETWORK: **FOX**
NORTH CAROLINA SPEEDWAY
ROCKINGHAM, N.C.
WWW.NORTHCAROLINASPEEDWAY.COM

**2003 WINNER:** Dale Jarrett
**FIRST RACE:** Oct. 31, 1965
**WINNER:** Curtis Turner
**QUALIFYING RECORD:** Rusty Wallace
158.035 mph, Feb. 25, 2000
**RACE RECORD:** Bobby Labonte
127.875 mph, Feb. 27, 2000
**MOST WINS:** 4, Richard Petty
**TRACK SPECS:** 1.017-mile oval, Turns 1–2
banked 22 degrees, Turns 3–4 banked
25 degrees
**TRACK FACT:** In 1969 North Carolina
Speedway became the first track to be
redesigned with the aid of a computer.

**DARRELL WALTRIP SAYS:** *There's
always a lot of sand on the track,
and this will eat up your tires.
To win you need excellent tire
management. Dale Jarrett will be
glad to get back to Rockingham.
This was the only race he won last
year—maybe he can get out of his
slump here.*

**ON THE BALL**
PEERING OUT OF THE
UNION 76 SPHERE, A
SPOTTER CHECKS
THE ACTION DURING
PRACTICE FOR THE
2003 DAYTONA 500.

PHOTOGRAPH BY
FRED VUICH

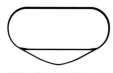

## Race 3

**UAW-DAIMLERCHRYSLER 400**
**MARCH 7, 2004**   NETWORK: **FOX**
LAS VEGAS MOTOR SPEEDWAY
LAS VEGAS, NEV.
WWW.LVMS.COM

**2003 WINNER:** Matt Kenseth
**FIRST RACE:** March 1, 1998
**WINNER:** Mark Martin
**QUALIFYING RECORD:** Bobby Labonte
173.016 mph, Feb. 28, 2003
**RACE RECORD:** Mark Martin
146.554 mph, March 1, 1998
**MOST WINS:** 2, Jeff Burton
**TRACK SPECS:** 1.5-mile oval, Turns 1–4 banked
12 degrees
**TRACK FACT:** This $200 million facility
opened in 1998 and it's not done: a 22,000-
seat grandstand, the Dale Earnhardt Terrace,
is set to open this year. In true Vegas fashion,
you can even get married during the race at this
track, known as the Diamond in the Desert.

**DARRELL WALTRIP SAYS:** *This is
Ryan Newman territory. The track
favors horsepower, and Newman is
always superior when it comes to
that. Matt Kenseth had his only
win of 2003 in Las Vegas, so he
should be a factor as well.*

## Race 4

**GOLDEN CORRAL 500**
**MARCH 14, 2004**   NETWORK: **FOX**
ATLANTA MOTOR SPEEDWAY
HAMPTON, GA.
WWW.ATLANTAMOTORSPEEDWAY.COM

**2003 WINNER:** Bobby Labonte
**FIRST RACE:** July 31, 1960
**WINNER:** Fireball Roberts
**QUALIFYING RECORD:** Bobby Labonte
194.957 mph, March 12, 1999
**RACE RECORD:** Dale Earnhardt
161.298 mph, March 10, 1996
**MOST WINS:** 6, Cale Yarborough
**TRACK SPECS:** 1.54-mile oval, Turns 1–4
banked 24 degrees
**TRACK FACT:** In 1997 the track was
reconfigured to include two short dogleg
turns, but a resurfacing helped keep it the
third-fastest raceway on the circuit—the
fastest without restrictor plates.

**DARRELL WALTRIP SAYS:** *This
track requires crew chiefs to go for
setups that produce excellent
handling because it's so fast.
Look for the Joe Gibbs cars here.
Bobby Labonte and Tony Stewart
are usually the guys to beat at
Atlanta.*

# March

**SHORT-TRACK PACK**
KENNY WALLACE (23) SPUN AND STACKED UP THE FIELD IN TYPICAL BRISTOL STYLE DURING THE FOOD CITY 500.

PHOTOGRAPH BY SAM SHARPE

## Race 5

### CAROLINA DODGE DEALERS 400

**MARCH 21, 2004**   NETWORK: **FOX**
DARLINGTON RACEWAY
DARLINGTON, S.C.
WWW.DARLINGTONRACEWAY.COM

**2003 WINNER:** Ricky Craven
**FIRST RACE:** Sept. 4, 1950
**WINNER:** Johnny Mantz
**QUALIFYING RECORD:** Ward Burton 173.797 mph, March 22, 1996
**RACE RECORD:** Dale Earnhardt 139.958 mph, March 28, 1993
**MOST WINS:** 7, David Pearson
**TRACK SPECS:** 1.366-mile oval, Turns 1–2 banked 25 degrees, Turns 3–4 banked 23 degrees
**TRACK FACT:** When Harold Brasington was building the track in the 1940s, he was forced to work around a pond that belonged to a farmer on an adjoining property, resulting in much tighter turns on the eastern end of the track than on the western end.

**DARRELL WALTRIP SAYS:** *The most exciting race of '03 took place here when Ricky Craven edged Kurt Busch by .002. Drivers who have a taken a lot of laps here—guys such as Terry Labonte and Bill Elliott— have an advantage.*

## Race 6

### FOOD CITY 500

**MARCH 28, 2004**   NETWORK: **FOX**
BRISTOL MOTOR SPEEDWAY
BRISTOL, TENN.
WWW.BRISTOLMOTORSPEEDWAY.COM

**2003 WINNER:** Kurt Busch
**FIRST RACE:** July 30, 1961
**WINNER:** Jack Smith
**QUALIFYING RECORD:** Ryan Newman 128.709 mph, March 23, 2003
**RACE RECORD:** Cale Yarborough 100.989 mph, April 17, 1977
**MOST WINS:** 6, Rusty Wallace
**TRACK SPECS:** .533-mile oval, Turns 1–4 banked 36 degrees
**TRACK FACT:** Bristol is the second shortest track on the Cup circuit. With its steep bankings and massive crowd, it is also the loudest spot in NASCAR.

**DARRELL WALTRIP SAYS:** *You gotta be a wild child to win here. There's so little time to react that you need to drive with reckless abandon. Clearly, the guy to beat is Kurt Busch. He's the kind of guy who is aggressive to the point where he'll take himself out. That's the attitude you need at Bristol.*

### Race 7
**SAMSUNG/RADIOSHACK 500**
**APRIL 4, 2004**   NETWORK: **FOX**
TEXAS MOTOR SPEEDWAY
JUSTIN, TEXAS
WWW.TEXASMOTORSPEEDWAY.COM

2003 WINNER: Ryan Newman
FIRST RACE: April 6, 1997
WINNER: Jeff Burton
QUALIFYING RECORD: Bill Elliott          RACE RECORD: Terry Labonte
194.224 mph, April 5, 2002          144.276 mph, March 28, 1999
MOST WINS: 1, Jeff Burton, Mark Martin, Terry Labonte, Dale Earnhardt Jr., Dale Jarrett, Matt Kenseth, Ryan Newman
TRACK SPECS: 1.5-mile oval, Turns 1–4 banked 24 degrees
TRACK FACT: The inaugural event here, in 1997, was a disaster, with 13 of the 43 starters involved in a wreck in the first lap.

DARRELL WALTRIP SAYS: *The drivers to watch out for at Texas are Jimmie Johnson and Ryan Newman. Both run their cars a lot looser than other drivers because they have the ability to hang on through the corners. This helps them get out of the turns real fast, which is what you need to do to win on this speedway.*

### Race 8
**ADVANCE AUTO PARTS 500**
**APRIL 18, 2004**   NETWORK: **FOX**
MARTINSVILLE SPEEDWAY
MARTINSVILLE, VA.
WWW.MARTINSVILLESPEEDWAY.COM

2003 WINNER: Jeff Gordon
FIRST RACE: May 20, 1956
WINNER: Buck Baker
QUALIFYING RECORD: Tony Stewart          RACE RECORD: Rusty Wallace
92.275 mph, April 16, 1999          81.410 mph, April 21, 1996
MOST WINS: 9, Richard Petty
TRACK SPECS: .526-mile oval, Turns 1–4 banked 12 degrees
TRACK FACT: NASCAR's oldest, slowest and smallest track, Martinsville is also the hardest on gears and fenders. It's like a bumper-car ride here, as drivers deliberately run into each other to slow down on the turns and conserve their brakes.

DARRELL WALTRIP SAYS: *This is a thinking man's race. There's always heavy traffic at Martinsville, so you need to force yourself to hold back a little; you can't just pound the car. The smarter drivers will be the ones to beat, guys like Jeff Gordon and Rusty Wallace.*

### Race 9
**AARON'S 499**
**APRIL 25, 2004**   NETWORK: **FOX**
TALLADEGA SUPERSPEEDWAY
TALLADEGA, ALA.
WWW.TALLADEGASUPERSPEEDWAY.COM

2003 WINNER: Dale Earnhardt Jr.
FIRST RACE: Sept. 14, 1969
WINNER: Richard Brickhouse
QUALIFYING RECORD: Bill Elliott          RACE RECORD: Mark Martin
212.809 mph, April 30, 1987          188.354 mph, May 10, 1997
MOST WINS: 6, Dale Earnhardt
TRACK SPECS: 2.66-mile tri-oval, Turns 1–4 banked 33 degrees, tri-oval banked 18 degrees
TRACK FACT: When Talladega opened in 1969, drivers discovered that their tires couldn't stand up to the extraordinarily high speeds achieved on this track, and they boycotted the race in a walkout led by Richard Petty.

DARRELL WALTRIP SAYS: *The racing here is always tight. The cars go around like a bunch of bumblebees. The DEI drivers have such a horsepower advantage at restrictor-plate races that the only way to beat them is when they beat themselves. But if anyone can, look for the Hendrick cars or Kevin Harvick.*

inston Cup Series

**JUST DANDY** THAT'S DEI'S MOTTO AT TALLADEGA, WHERE MICHAEL WALTRIP AND DALE EARNHARDT JR. HAVE WON THE LAST FIVE RACES.

PHOTOGRAPH BY JONATHAN FERREY/GETTY IMAGES

# May

## Race 10

### AUTO CLUB 500
**MAY 2, 2004**   NETWORK: **FOX**
CALIFORNIA SPEEDWAY
FONTANA, CALIF.
WWW.CALIFORNIASPEEDWAY.COM

2003 WINNER: Kurt Busch
FIRST RACE: June 22, 1997
WINNER: Jeff Gordon
QUALIFYING RECORD: Ryan Newman          RACE RECORD: Jeff Gordon
187.432 mph, April 26, 2002                     155.012 mph, June 22, 1997
MOST WINS: 2, Jeff Gordon
TRACK SPECS: 2.0-mile oval, Turns 1–4 banked 14 degrees
TRACK FACT: In an unprecedented move NASCAR issued the California Speedway a Winston Cup race date before Roger Penske even broke ground for the new facility.

DARRELL WALTRIP SAYS: *This is another Ryan Newman track. He keeps it mashed all day long on this sister track of Michigan's. It's a wide track, so there should be plenty of side-by-side racing. You can also see some heavy crashes. Dale Jr.'s slam into the wall in 2002 was one of the hardest impacts I've ever seen.*

## Race 11

### PONTIAC PERFORMANCE 400
**MAY 15, 2004**   NETWORK: **FX**
RICHMOND INTERNATIONAL RACEWAY
RICHMOND, VA.
WWW.RIR.COM

2003 WINNER: Joe Nemechek
FIRST RACE: April 19, 1953
WINNER: Lee Petty
QUALIFYING RECORD: Ward Burton          RACE RECORD: Rusty Wallace
127.389 mph, May 4, 2002                      108.499 mph, March 2, 1997
MOST WINS: 6, Lee Petty
TRACK SPECS: .750-mile oval, Turns 1–4 banked 14 degrees
TRACK FACT: Racing at Richmond, which began in 1946, predates NASCAR. Once known as Strawberry Hill Raceway, the track had a surface so bumpy that drivers claimed the name came from fruit being picked off it the night before the race.

DARRELL WALTRIP SAYS: *Richmond'll fool you. It's faster than you think. It's a short track with superspeedway kind of speed. Coming off Turn 4 you pick up a lot of speed and you don't want to have a problem going into Turn 1, because you can really take a hard lick there.*

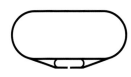

## Race 12

### COCA-COLA 600
**MAY 30, 2004**   NETWORK: **FOX**
LOWE'S MOTOR SPEEDWAY
CONCORD, N.C.
WWW.LOWESMOTORSPEEDWAY.COM

2003 WINNER: Jimmie Johnson
FIRST RACE: June 19, 1960
WINNER: Joe Lee Johnson
QUALIFYING RECORD: Jimmie Johnson          RACE RECORD: Bobby Labonte
186.464 mph, May 23, 2002                        151.952 mph, May 28, 1995
MOST WINS: 5, Darrell Waltrip
TRACK SPECS: 1.5-mile oval, Turns 1–4 banked 24 degrees
TRACK FACT: While track conditions at Lowe's are generally good, there's a notorious bump coming off Turn 4 known in the industry as the Humpy Bump, in honor of the track's president, H.A. (Humpy) Wheeler.

DARRELL WALTRIP SAYS: *The track at Charlotte is rough, and the cars bounce around, but the drivers don't seem to mind, because they've driven here so many times. This is another Joe Gibbs track. His operation has had a good setup here for years, so look for either Bobby Labonte or Tony Stewart—or both—to run near the front.*

 Race 13

## MBNA AMERICA 400
**JUNE 6, 2004** NETWORK: **FX**
DOVER INTERNATIONAL SPEEDWAY
DOVER, DEL.
WWW.DOVERSPEEDWAY.COM

2003 WINNER: Ryan Newman
FIRST RACE: July 6, 1969
WINNER: Richard Petty
QUALIFYING RECORD: Bobby Labonte
159.320 mph, June 4, 1999
RACE RECORD: Bobby Labonte
120.603 mph, June 6, 1999
MOST WINS: 5, Bobby Allison
TRACK SPECS: 1-mile oval, Turns 1–4
banked 24 degrees
TRACK FACT: For 16 consecutive years
Dover's owners expanded the grandstands
at the speedway, increasing its capacity
from 22,000 in 1985 to the current
140,000.

DARRELL WALTRIP SAYS: *This track
is paved with concrete. It used to
be very rough, but it's smoothed
out some over the years. You
should be able to pick the winner
at Dover out of these four drivers:
Jimmie Johnson, Jeff Gordon,
Ryan Newman and Tony Stewart.*

 Race 14

## POCONO 500
**JUNE 13, 2004** NETWORK: **FOX**
POCONO RACEWAY
LONG POND, PA.
WWW.POCONORACEWAY.COM

2003 WINNER: Tony Stewart
FIRST RACE: August 5, 1974
WINNER: Richard Petty
QUALIFYING RECORD: Rusty Wallace
171.625 mph, June 17, 2000
RACE RECORD: Alan Kulwicki
144.023 mph, June 14, 1992
MOST WINS: 2, Jeff Gordon
TRACK SPECS: 2.5-mile oval, Turn 1 banked
14 degrees, Turn 2 banked 8 degrees, Turn 3
banked 6 degrees
TRACK FACT: The varying turns on this
triangular course make it hard for an
accurate chassis setup, and the gear
specialists become frustrated with the
different straightaway lengths.

DARRELL WALTRIP SAYS: *This is not
a physically draining race, but it's
hard on equipment. The long
backstraight puts a lot of stress on
the transmission, so you'll get engine
failures. The winner here usually
has a lot of horsepower—right up
Ryan Newman's alley.*

**HARD RIGHT**
INFINEON'S WINDING
ROAD COURSE
ALWAYS HAS DRIVERS
GOING IN ALL SORTS
OF UNFAMILIAR
DIRECTIONS.

PHOTOGRAPH BY
DONALD MIRALLE/GETTY IMAGES

 **Race 15**

## MICHIGAN 400
**JUNE 20, 2004**   NETWORK: **FOX**
MICHIGAN INTERNATIONAL SPEEDWAY
BROOKLYN, MICH.
WWW.MISPEEDWAY.COM

**2003 WINNER:** Kurt Busch
**FIRST RACE:** June 15, 1969
**WINNER:** Cale Yarborough
**QUALIFYING RECORD:** Bobby Labonte
190.365 mph, June 13, 2003
**RACE RECORD:** Dale Jarrett
173.997 mph, June 13, 1999
**MOST WINS:** 6, Cale Yarborough
**TRACK SPECS:** 2-mile oval, Turns 1–4
banked 18 degrees
**TRACK FACT:** Races at Michigan Speedway
hold extra incentive for drivers, who are
watched carefully by the carmakers'
engineers and executives from Detroit.

**DARRELL WALTRIP SAYS:** *Like
California, this is a track that will
lose grip. To win, you must have a
fast, good-handling car. Bill Elliott
used to dominate Michigan, but
these days the two guys who are
good at making speed and
handling their car at this track are
Tony Stewart and Bobby Labonte.*

 **Race 16**

## DODGE/SAVE MART 350
**JUNE 27, 2004**   NETWORK: **FOX**
INFINEON RACEWAY
SONOMA, CALIF.
WWW.INFINEONRACEWAY.COM

**2003 WINNER:** Robby Gordon
**FIRST RACE:** June 11, 1989
**WINNER:** Ricky Rudd
**QUALIFYING RECORD:** Jeff Gordon
93.699 mph, June 22, 2001
**RACE RECORD:** Ricky Rudd
81.007 mph, June 23, 2002
**MOST WINS:** 3, Jeff Gordon
**TRACK SPECS:** 2-mile road course
**TRACK FACT:** In 1998 Turns 4 through 7 were
connected to make one straightaway called
the Chute, which allowed fans a better view of
the action and drivers a better chance to
battle for position before the next turn.

**DARRELL WALTRIP SAYS:** *On this
course you're constantly breaking,
shifting, going left, going right.
Hired guns such as Boris Said and
Ron Fellows have been coming in
and doing well recently. You've got
to manhandle your car here, and
no regular NASCAR driver is better
at this than Robby Gordon.*

## Race 17
### PEPSI 400
**JULY 3, 2004**  NETWORK: **FOX**
DAYTONA INTERNATIONAL SPEEDWAY
DAYTONA BEACH, FLA.
WWW.DAYTONAINTLSPEEDWAY.COM

**2003 WINNER:** Greg Biffle
**FIRST RACE:** Feb. 22, 1959
**WINNER:** Lee Petty
**QUALIFYING RECORD:** Sterling Marlin
203.666 mph, July 3, 1986
**RACE RECORD:** Bobby Allison
173.473 mph, July 4, 1980
**MOST WINS:** 5, David Pearson
**TRACK SPECS:** 2.5-mile oval, Turns 1–4 banked 31 degrees, tri-oval
banked 18 degrees
**TRACK FACT:** Daytona Beach is the center of the stock car racing world and home to
NASCAR's official attraction, Daytona USA (picture Disney World for race fans).
While cars on the track are slowed to under 200 mph by restrictor plates, a land
speed record of 276 mph was set on Daytona Beach in 1935 by Sir Malcolm Campbell.

**DARRELL WALTRIP SAYS:** *This race is at night so, even though it's
July, the conditions are similar to February. This makes it easier for
the crew chief because he can rely on his notes. Like February, it's
going to take a huge effort to beat Michael and Dale Jr.*

## Race 18
### TROPICANA 400
**JULY 11, 2004**  NETWORK: **NBC**
CHICAGOLAND SPEEDWAY
JOLIET, ILL.
WWW.CHICAGOLANDSPEEDWAY.COM

**2003 WINNER:** Ryan Newman
**FIRST RACE:** July 15, 2001
**WINNER:** Kevin Harvick
**QUALIFYING RECORD:** Tony Stewart
184.786 mph, July 11, 2003
**RACE RECORD:** Kevin Harvick
136.832 mph, July 14, 2002
**MOST WINS:** 2, Kevin Harvick
**TRACK SPECS:** 1.5-mile tri-oval, Turns 1–4 banked 18 degrees
**TRACK FACT:** What makes Chicagoland unique is the bowed backstretch, which
perpetuates the feeling of constant turning instead of the normal rhythm of
straightaway, turn, straightaway.

**DARRELL WALTRIP SAYS:** *The rap on this track and on Kansas
City, which also opened in 2001, is that they've only got one real
groove. Drivers must run on the bottom, and if they get out of
the groove they crash. There's not a lot of side-by-side racing,
but it can get exciting when guys try to root each other out of
the groove.*

## Race 19
### NEW ENGLAND 300
**JULY 25, 2004**  NETWORK: **TNT**
NEW HAMPSHIRE INTERNATIONAL SPEEDWAY
LOUDON, N.H.
WWW.NHIS.COM

**2003 WINNER:** Jimmie Johnson
**FIRST RACE:** July 11, 1993
**WINNER:** Rusty Wallace
**QUALIFYING RECORD:** Rusty Wallace
132.089 mph, July 7, 2000
**RACE RECORD:** Jeff Burton
117.134 mph, July 13, 1997
**MOST WINS:** 3, Jeff Burton
**TRACK SPECS:** 1.058-mile oval, Turns 1–4 banked 12 degrees
**TRACK FACT:** The New Hampshire track was formerly the site of a motorcycle road
circuit and has low bankings and a paper-clip shape that traditionally made
passing difficult; recent resurfacing has made for better racing.

**DARRELL WALTRIP SAYS:** *This is a one-mile track that has
short-track tendencies. It's very tough to get comfortable here
because on the long straightaways you generate a lot of speed
and then you have to take the sharp, nearly flat turns. The
drivers to watch here are the two Hendrick boys, Jimmie
Johnson and Jeff Gordon.*

# July

**STILL GREEN** JUST
THREE YEARS OLD,
CHICAGOLAND
HASN'T GOT ITS
SECOND GROOVE
YET, WHICH LIMITS
SIDE-BY-SIDE RACING.

PHOTOGRAPH BY
BRIAN CLEARY/ICON SMI

Race 20

## PENNSYLVANIA 500
**AUGUST 1, 2004**   NETWORK: **TNT**
POCONO RACEWAY
LONG POND, PA.
WWW.POCONORACEWAY.COM

**2003 WINNER:** Ryan Newman
**FIRST RACE:** Aug. 5, 1974
**WINNER:** Richard Petty
**QUALIFYING RECORD:** Tony Stewart
172.391 mph, July 21, 2000
**RACE RECORD:** Rusty Wallace
144.892 mph, July 21, 1996
**MOST WINS:** 4, Bill Elliott
**TRACK SPECS:** 2.5-mile oval, Turn 1 banked
14 degrees, Turn 2 banked 8 degrees, Turn 3
banked 6 degrees
**TRACK FACT:** The two Pocono NASCAR
races are only six weeks apart—the shortest
interval between any of the races at the same
track during the season.

**DARRELL WALTRIP SAYS:** *The track
is a little different this time around.
It's been laying there all summer
and now it's slicker, which will force
teams to change setups. Ryan
Newman has to be favored. His
engine can generate high RPMs on
the long straightaways.*

Race 21

## BRICKYARD 400
**AUGUST 8, 2004**   NETWORK: **NBC**
INDIANAPOLIS MOTOR SPEEDWAY
INDIANAPOLIS, IND.
WWW.BRICKYARD400.COM

**2003 WINNER:** Kevin Harvick
**FIRST RACE:** (Brickyard 400) Aug. 6, 1994
**WINNER:** Jeff Gordon
**QUALIFYING RECORD:** Kevin Harvick
184.343 mph, Aug. 2, 2003
**RACE RECORD:** Bobby Labonte
155.912 mph, Aug. 5, 2000
**MOST WINS:** 3, Jeff Gordon
**TRACK SPECS:** 2.5-mile oval, Turns 1–4
banked 9 degrees
**TRACK FACT:** More than a million race fans
applied for the 300,000 tickets available in
1994 when Indy opened to Winston Cup.
Those fans were in Hoosier Heaven when they
saw native son Jeff Gordon win the race and
spend nearly an hour in Victory Lane.

**DARRELL WALTRIP SAYS:** *This is
my favorite race. The Daytona 500
defines the sport, but I have more
passion for this race because there's
so much history at Indy. You must
have finesse at Indy; you can't
attack the track. At Indy you need
to slow down to go fast.*

August

**ESS-DAY TEST**

WHEN THEY RACE AT WATKINS GLEN, ONCE THE SITE OF THE U.S. GRAND PRIX, NASCAR DRIVERS ARE GRADED ON A CURVE (OR TWO).

PHOTOGRAPH BY
BRIAN SPURLOCK

## Race 22
SIRIUS AT THE GLEN
**AUGUST 15, 2004**   NETWORK: **TNT**
WATKINS GLEN INTERNATIONAL
WATKINS GLEN, N.Y.
WWW.THEGLEN.COM

2003 WINNER: Robby Gordon
FIRST RACE: Aug. 4, 1957
WINNER: Buck Baker
QUALIFYING RECORD: Jeff Gordon        RACE RECORD: Mark Martin
124.580 mph, Aug. 8, 2003               103.030 mph, Aug. 13, 1995
MOST WINS: 4, Jeff Gordon
TRACK SPECS: 2.45-mile road course, banks range from 6 to 10 degrees
TRACK FACT: Law student Cameron Argetsinger drew up the course in 1948 in a quest to bring European-style sports car racing to the village in which he spent his summer vacations. The original track was laid out over asphalt, concrete and dirt roads.

DARRELL WALTRIP SAYS: *The second road course on the NASCAR circuit, the Glen is a fast, sweeping racetrack. The key is to stay on the track. If you go off, you'll either hit something or get stuck in the kitty litter. The guy to watch is Robby Gordon, who won both road races in '03.*

## Race 23
MICHIGAN 400
**AUGUST 22, 2004**   NETWORK: **TNT**
MICHIGAN INTERNATIONAL SPEEDWAY
BROOKLYN, MICH.
WWW.MISPEEDWAY.COM

FIRST RACE: June 15, 1969
WINNER: Cale Yarborough
2003 WINNER: Ryan Newman
QUALIFYING RECORD: Dale Earnhardt Jr.   RACE RECORD: Bobby Labonte
191.149 mph, Aug. 18, 2000              157.739 mph, August 20, 1995
MOST WINS: 5, David Pearson
TRACK SPECS: 2-mile oval, Turns 1-4 banked 18 degrees
TRACK FACT: Michigan International Speedway was a symbol of a new era of prosperity for the Irish Hills area near Detroit when it opened in 1968, boasting 25,983 seats. Gradual renovations have been made since then, and reserved seating capacity is now 136,373.

DARRELL WALTRIP SAYS: *The conditions are different the second time around. The IRL runs here a week before, and that race leaves a lot of oil on the track, so it doesn't have the grip it had in June. You can have some surprise names running in the front here, because the setup is often hit or miss.*

## Race 24
SHARPIE 500
**AUGUST 28, 2004**   NETWORK: **TNT**
BRISTOL MOTOR SPEEDWAY
BRISTOL, TENN.
WWW. BRISTOLMOTORSPEEDWAY.COM

2003 WINNER: Kurt Busch
FIRST RACE: July 30, 1961
WINNER: Jack Smith
QUALIFYING RECORD: Jeff Gordon        RACE RECORD: Charlie Glotzbach
127.597 mph, Aug. 23, 2003             101.074 mph, July 11, 1971
MOST WINS: 7, Darrell Waltrip
TRACK SPECS: .533-mile oval, Turns 1-4 banked 36 degrees
TRACK FACT: Jack Smith won the inaugural event at Bristol but wasn't behind the wheel for the checkered flag. He drove the first 290 laps but needed relief driver Johnny Allen to take over for the final 210. They shared the $3,225 purse.

DARRELL WALTRIP SAYS: *It's hot in Tennessee in August, and this race will absolutely suck the air and the life right out of you. With 43 cars running round on such a tight track, you have to concentrate on not getting caught up in a wreck early in the race and wait until the field is thinned out by 10 or so cars before going to work.*

**Race 25**

## POP SECRET 500
**SEPTEMBER 5, 2004**   **NETWORK: NBC**
CALIFORNIA SPEEDWAY
FONTANA, CALIF.
WWW.CALIFORNIASPEEDWAY.COM

**2003 WINNER:** N.A. (New September race)
**FIRST RACE:** June 22, 1997
**WINNER:** Jeff Gordon
**QUALIFYING RECORD:** Ryan Newman
187.432 mph, April 26, 2002
**RACE RECORD:** Jeff Gordon
155.012 mph, June 22, 1997
**MOST WINS:** 2, Jeff Gordon
**TRACK SPECS:** 2.0-mile oval, Turns 1–4
banked 14 degrees
**TRACK FACT:** California's D-shaped oval
accommodates up to five cars across, which
allows for many different leaders during a
race. During the inaugural race, in 1997, Jeff
Gordon swapped the lead with other drivers
21 times before pulling out the victory.

**DARRELL WALTRIP SAYS:** *This will
be the first NASCAR night race at
California Speedway, as well as the
first time the circuit has visited the
track twice in one season. Because
no one knows what conditions will
be like at night, you could have a
surprise winner here.*

**Race 26**

## CHEVY MONTE CARLO 400
**SEPTEMBER 11, 2004**   **NETWORK: TNT**
RICHMOND INTERNATIONAL RACEWAY
RICHMOND, VA.
WWW.RIR.COM

**2003 WINNER:** Ryan Newman
**FIRST RACE:** April 19, 1953
**WINNER:** Lee Petty
**QUALIFYING RECORD:** Jimmie Johnson
126.145 mph, Sept. 6, 2002
**RACE RECORD:** Dale Jarrett
109.047 mph,  Sept. 6, 1997
**MOST WINS:** 6, Richard Petty
**TRACK SPECS:** .75-mile oval, Turns 1–4
banked 14 degrees
**TRACK FACT:** The original track on the site
of the State Fairgrounds was razed in 1988
after Richard Petty climbed aboard a
bulldozer and ceremoniously ripped up a
portion of the first turn.

**DARRELL WALTRIP SAYS:** *There's no
change in track conditions from
the first race, though it will be
hotter. There have been a lot of
heavy impacts here—Jerry Nadeau's
wreck last year, for instance—but
the new safe barriers seem to be
doing the job.*

# September

ROCK-RIBBED RACIN'
THE ACTION ON THE
FLAT TRACK AT
LOUDON DRAWS
RABID NASCAR FANS
FROM ALL OVER
NEW ENGLAND.

PHOTOGRAPH BY
MICHAEL J. LEBRECHT II

 Race 27

SYLVANIA 300
**SEPTEMBER 19, 2004**   NETWORK: **TNT**
NEW HAMPSHIRE INTERNATIONAL SPEEDWAY
LOUDON, N.H.
WWW.NHIS.COM

**2003 WINNER:** Jimmie Johnson
**FIRST RACE:** July 11, 1993
**WINNER:** Rusty Wallace
**QUALIFYING RECORD:** Ryan Newman
133.357 mph, Sept. 14, 2003
**RACE RECORD:** Jeff Gordon
112.078 mph, Aug. 28, 1998
**MOST WINS:** 3, Jeff Burton
**TRACK SPECS:** 1.058-mile oval, Turns 1–4
banked 12 degrees
**TRACK FACT:** The staff at NHIS believe in
keeping up appearances—even after
practice rounds they paint over all the
scuff marks, sometimes requiring up to 33
gallons of paint for one day of racing.

DARRELL WALTRIP SAYS: *The key
here is the sealer that they put on
the track. It's fine when it's fresh,
but before the Nextel Cup boys run
on Sunday, a modified race, a Busch
North race and a truck race will
wear the sealer down. You have to
anticipate the change in conditions.*

 Race 28

MBNA AMERICA 400
**SEPTEMBER 26, 2004**   NETWORK: **TNT**
DOVER INTERNATIONAL SPEEDWAY
DOVER, DEL.
WWW.DOVERSPEEDWAY.COM

**2003 WINNER:** Ryan Newman
**FIRST RACE:** July 6, 1969
**WINNER:** Richard Petty
**QUALIFYING RECORD:** Rusty Wallace
159.964 mph, Sept. 24, 1999
**RACE RECORD:** Mark Martin
132.719 mph, Sept. 21, 1997
**MOST WINS:** 4, Richard Petty
**TRACK SPECS:** 1.0-mile oval, Turns 1–4
banked 24 degrees
**TRACK FACT:** Dover Downs got its name
because it was built around a horse racing
track on the former site of the Delaware
State Police barracks.

DARRELL WALTRIP SAYS: *The track
won't change much from the first
race, so a crew chief can basically
go with the same setup. Because
of this, don't be surprised if
the same driver wins both races
at Dover. Jimmie Johnson did it
in 2002, and he might do it again
this year.*

**Race 29**

## EA SPORTS 500
**OCTOBER 3, 2004**   NETWORK: **NBC**
TALLADEGA SUPERSPEEDWAY
TALLADEGA, ALA.
WWW.TALLADEGASUPERSPEEDWAY.COM

**2003 WINNER:** Michael Waltrip
**FIRST RACE:** Sept. 14, 1969
**WINNER:** Richard Brickhouse
**QUALIFYING RECORD:** Bill Elliott
209.005 mph, July 24, 1986
**RACE RECORD:** Dale Earnhardt Jr.
183.665 mph, Oct. 6, 2002
**MOST WINS:** 4, Dale Earnhardt
**TRACK SPECS:** 2.66-mile tri-oval,
Turns 1–4 banked 33 degrees, tri-oval
banked 18 degrees
**TRACK FACT:** In 1987 a fan threw a beer can
onto the track that cut Bobby Allison's tire,
sending his car airborne at more than
200 mph. It tore down a 150-foot stretch of
fence along the grandstands (Allison was
O.K.). As a result, restrictor plates were
imposed to keep speeds below 200.

DARRELL WALTRIP SAYS: *It's
simple here: You must beat DEI.
And there's four drivers who have
both the resources and talent to do
that: Jimmie Johnson, Jeff Gordon,
Tony Stewart and Ryan Newman.*

**Race 30**

## BANQUET 400 PRESENTED BY CONAGRA FOODS
**OCTOBER 10, 2004**   NETWORK: **NBC**
KANSAS SPEEDWAY
KANSAS CITY, KANS.
WWW.KANSASSPEEDWAY.COM

**2003 WINNER:** Ryan Newman
**FIRST RACE:** Sept. 30, 2001
**WINNER:** Jeff Gordon
**QUALIFYING RECORD:** Jimmie Johnson
180.373 mph, Oct. 3, 2003
**RACE RECORD:** Ryan Newman
121.630 mph, Oct. 5, 2003
**MOST WINS:** 2, Jeff Gordon
**TRACK SPECS:** 1.5-mile tri-oval, Turns 1–4
banked 15 degrees
**TRACK FACT:** Race fans who make a $75
charitable donation can have a NASCAR-
related message carved in a brick and set
into the pavement at the speedway entrance.

DARRELL WALTRIP SAYS: *This track
lacks grip and is really, really fast.
The biggest driver complaint is
that, like Chicago, there's only one
groove. And because it's so new
guys are still searching for the right
setup. Ryan Newman won here last
year, which to me makes him the
favorite this year.*

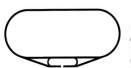

## Race 31
**UAW-GM QUALITY 500**
**OCTOBER 16, 2004** **NETWORK: NBC**
LOWE'S MOTOR SPEEDWAY
CONCORD, N.C.
WWW.LOWESMOTORSPEEDWAY.COM

**2003 WINNER:** Tony Stewart
**FIRST RACE:** June 19, 1960
**WINNER:** Joe Lee Johnson
**QUALIFYING RECORD:** Ryan Newman
186.657 mph, Oct. 9, 2003
**RACE RECORD:** Jeff Gordon
160.306 mph, Oct. 11, 1999
**MOST WINS:** 3, Mark Martin
**TRACK SPECS:** 1.5-mile oval, Turns 1–4 banked 24 degrees
**TRACK FACT:** In 1961 Junior Johnson broke two axles, so a fan went out to his own car in the parking lot, removed the axle and gave it to Johnson so that he could finish the race. Johnson broke that axle too. In keeping with that spirit of fan loyalty, in 1984 Lowe's became the first sports facility in the U.S. to offer permanent accommodations to racegoers when the track began selling condominiums above Turn 1.

**DARRELL WALTRIP SAYS:** *Crew chiefs can use their notes from May to figure out their setup. Both races are at night, so the track conditions will be similar. Like the other races at Lowe's, watch out for the Gibbs cars.*

## Race 32
**SUBWAY 500**
**OCTOBER 24, 2004** **NETWORK: NBC**
MARTINSVILLE SPEEDWAY
MARTINSVILLE, VA
WWW.MARTINSVILLESPEEDWAY.COM

**2003 WINNER:** Jeff Gordon
**FIRST RACE:** May 20, 1956
**WINNER:** Buck Baker
**QUALIFYING RECORD:** Tony Stewart
95.371 mph, Sept. 30, 2000
**RACE RECORD:** Jeff Gordon
82.223 mph, Sept. 22, 1996
**MOST WINS:** 6, Richard Petty
**TRACK SPECS:** .526-mile oval, Turns 1–4 banked 12 degrees
**TRACK FACT:** In the early 1950s Martinsville builder Clay Earles thought the outhouses in the infield weren't fit for women to look at, so he had them covered with climbing roses, which caused a substantial number of bees to swarm and more than one spectator to flee with his pants down.

**DARRELL WALTRIP SAYS:** *At Martinsville it's almost like you're stuck in stop-and-go traffic on the interstate. You have to ride the breaks, so you're always on them. You gotta be careful not to burn your brakes off. The winner here is usually the guy who takes the best care of his car.*

## Race 33
**BASS PRO SHOPS MBNA 500**
**OCTOBER 31, 2004** **NETWORK: NBC**
ATLANTA MOTOR SPEEDWAY
HAMPTON, GA.
WWW.ATLANTAMOTORSPEEDWAY.COM

**2003 WINNER:** Jeff Gordon
**FIRST RACE:** July 31, 1960
**WINNER:** Fireball Roberts
**QUALIFYING RECORD:** Geoffrey Bodine
197.478 mph, Nov. 15, 1997
**RACE RECORD:** Dale Earnhardt
163.633 mph, Nov. 12, 1995
**MOST WINS:** 4, Bobby Labonte
**TRACK SPECS:** 1.54-mile oval, Turns 1–4 banked 24 degrees
**TRACK FACT:** Onetime Atlanta Speedway ticket vendor Jimmy Carter, while running for governor of Georgia, promised to host a barbecue dinner at the state house for the Speedway community if he won, a pledge he upheld upon his election. Later, as president, he threw a NASCAR bash at the White House, complete with stock cars circling the driveway, Willie Nelson singing and Rosalynn Carter waving a racing flag. Offered attendee Junior Johnson, "[NASCAR]'s getting sort of sophisticated-like."

**DARRELL WALTRIP SAYS:** *If a Roush or Hendrick car doesn't win here, I'd be surprised. The other driver to watch is Dale Earnhardt Jr., who last season had two finishes in the top six at Atlanta.*

**CAUTIONARY TALE**
FREQUENT FLAGS AND CRASHES ARE A BIG REASON WHY 11 DRIVERS HAVE WON THE LAST 13 RACES AT MARTINSVILLE.

PHOTOGRAPH BY
AL MESSERSCHMIDT/WIREIMAGE.COM

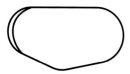

## Race 34
### CHECKER AUTO PARTS 500
**NOVEMBER 7, 2004** NETWORK: **NBC**
PHOENIX INTERNATIONAL RACEWAY
PHOENIX, ARIZ.
WWW.PHOENIXINTLRACEWAY.COM

**2003 WINNER:** Dale Earnhardt Jr.
**FIRST RACE:** Nov. 6, 1988
**WINNER:** Alan Kulwicki
**QUALIFYING RECORD:** Rusty Wallace 134.178 mph, Nov. 3, 2000
**RACE RECORD:** Tony Stewart 118.132 mph, Nov. 7, 1999
**MOST WINS:** 2, Davey Allison and Jeff Burton
**TRACK SPECS:** 1-mile oval, Turns 1–2 banked 11 degrees, Turns 3–4 banked 9 degrees
**TRACK FACT:** When Alan Kulwicki won the first race at Phoenix, he made a U-turn after passing the checkered flag and circled the track clockwise in what he later called his "Polish victory lap."

**DARRELL WALTRIP SAYS:** *There's always tight racing here. You gotta be careful coming off Turn 2; you see a lot of guys hit the wall there. The winner is usually excellent at handling his car, and he's got high horsepower—two reasons why this is a Matt Kenseth type of track.*

## Race 35
### MOUNTAIN DEW SOUTHERN 500
**NOVEMBER 14, 2004** NETWORK: **NBC**
DARLINGTON RACEWAY
DARLINGTON, S.C.
WWW.DARLINGTONRACEWAY.COM

**2003 WINNER:** Bill Elliott
**FIRST RACE:** Sept. 4, 1950
**WINNER:** Johnny Mantz
**QUALIFYING RECORD:** Kenny Irwin 170.970 mph, Sept. 3, 1999
**RACE RECORD:** Jeff Gordon 139.031 mph, Sept. 6, 1998
**MOST WINS:** 5, Cale Yarborough
**TRACK SPECS:** 1.366-mile oval, Turns 1–2 banked 25 degrees, Turns 3–4 banked 23 degrees
**TRACK FACT:** Darlington has been personified as the Lady in Black. Dale Earnhardt said, after he hit the wall on the way to victory in the 1990 Southern 500, one of his nine wins in total here, "You seen her reach out and slap me today when I got fresh with her, didn't you?"

**DARRELL WALTRIP SAYS:** *The track is the real competition at Darlington. Guys who remember that do well. It's a long race, 500 miles, so you gotta be patient. Terry Labonte has always done well here, so he's my guy to watch.*

## Race 36
### FORD 400
**NOVEMBER 21, 2004** NETWORK: **NBC**
HOMESTEAD-MIAMI SPEEDWAY
HOMESTEAD, FLA.
WWW.HOMESTEADMIAMISPEEDWAY.COM

**2003 WINNER:** Bobby Labonte
**FIRST RACE:** Nov. 14, 1999
**WINNER:** Tony Stewart
**QUALIFYING RECORD:** Jamie McMurray 181.111 mph, Nov. 16, 2003
**RACE RECORD:** Tony Stewart 140.335 mph, Nov. 14, 1999
**MOST WINS:** 2, Tony Stewart
**TRACK SPECS:** 1.5-mile oval, Turns 1–4 banked 6 degrees
**TRACK FACT:** This smooth and wide track opened in 1994 and was initially built to help boost South Florida's economy, which had been damaged by Hurricane Andrew in '92 and the subsequent closing of Homestead Air Force base.

**DARRELL WALTRIP SAYS:** *Last year Homestead underwent its fourth design change, so drivers and teams will likely find that it's still somewhat unpredictable. Because of that, if I'm trying to win the championship, I don't want it to come down to being decided on this track. There's too many opportunities for things to go wrong.*

**DESERT BLOOM** A SHORT TRACK WITH SUPERSPEEDWAY SIZZLE, PHOENIX HAS SHONE BRIGHTLY IN THE VALLEY OF THE SUN SINCE 1988.

PHOTOGRAPH BY RICK HOSSMAN/AP

November

**MAN IN THE MIRROR**
THAT WOULD BE
RYAN NEWMAN, OUR
PICK TO WIN THE
2004 NEXTEL CUP.

# 2004
# SCOUTING REPORTS

## How We Rank The Drivers

PHOTOGRAPH BY SAM SHARPE

1. Ryan **NEWMAN**
2. Jeff **GORDON**
3. Dale **EARNHARDT Jr.**
4. Jimmie **JOHNSON**
5. Kurt **BUSCH**
6. Matt **KENSETH**
7. Kevin **HARVICK**
8. Tony **STEWART**
9. Bobby **LABONTE**
10. Robby **GORDON**
11. Michael **WALTRIP**
12. Jamie **McMURRAY**
13. Rusty **WALLACE**
14. Sterling **MARLIN**
15. Jeff **BURTON**
16. Terry **LABONTE**
17. Mark **MARTIN**
18. Ward **BURTON**
19. Brian **VICKERS**
20. Greg **BIFFLE**

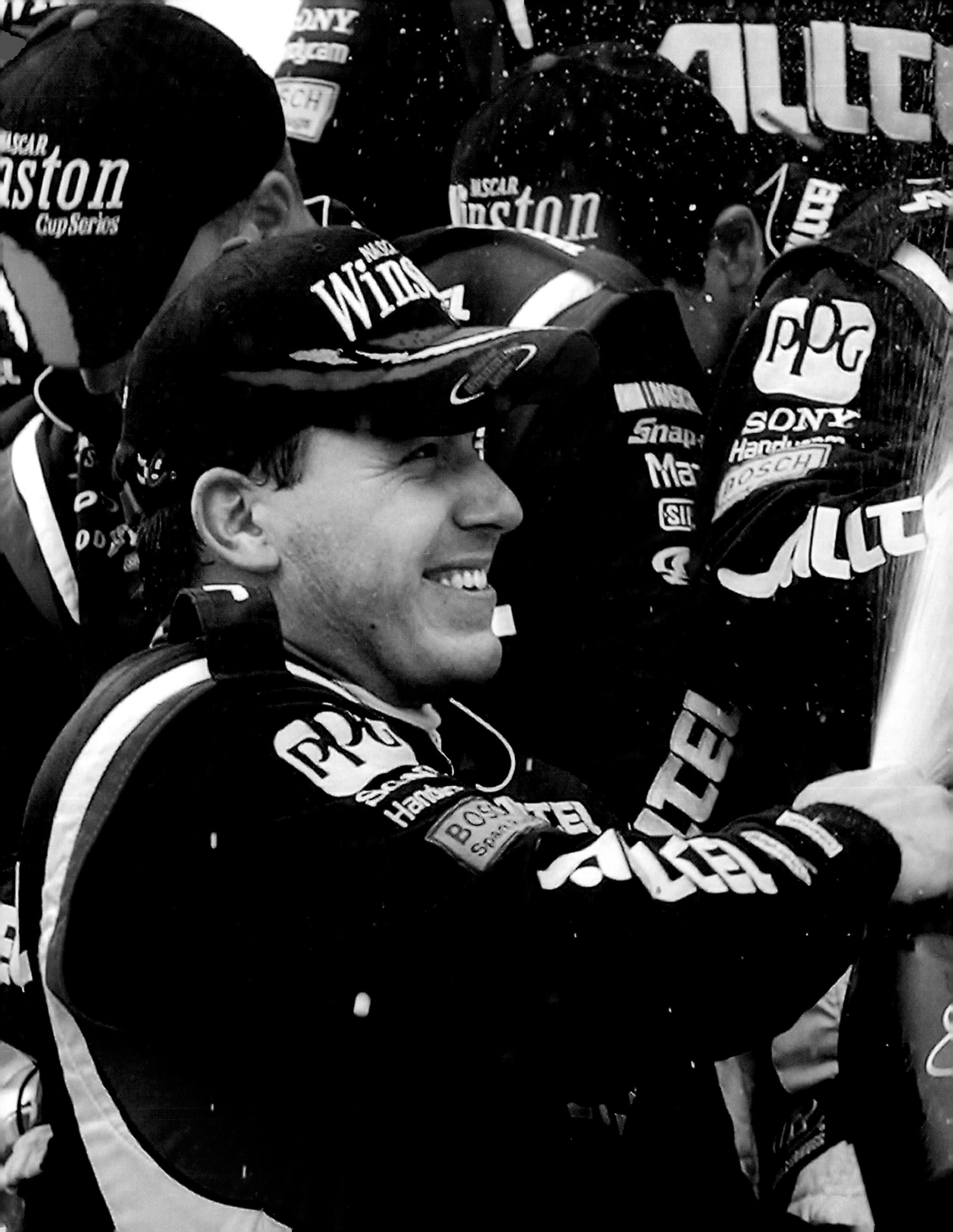
NASCAR
Cup Series
PPG
SONY
BOSCH

IF AMERICA truly wants to break its dependence on foreign oil, maybe it should consider making Ryan Newman the energy czar. At least that's the conclusion one could draw from listening to his fellow drivers. Last season Newman, crew chief Matt Borland and chief engineer Mike Nelson squeezed every last drop out of the standard 22-gallon tank as Newman won a circuit-high eight races, four more than anyone else. The question was, How'd they do it?

Some rivals claimed they'd been outsmarted by slide-rule-wielding geeks. When fellow Dodge driver Jeremy Mayfield was asked to explain the number 12 team's mastery of fuel economy, he sniffed, "I'm not an engineer." Newman, who graduated from Purdue University in 2001 with a B.S. in Vehicle Structural Engineering, famously is; so are Borland and Nelson. Other drivers were less polite, claiming that Newman's uncanny ability to drive farther than they could on the same amount of gas wasn't due to careful calculations by Nelson and Borland or cautious handling by Newman but to, well, simple cheating. "If he can do that with his foot, then he's a magician," said Kevin Harvick. "I'll kiss his ass if he's doing it with his foot." Added Tony Stewart, "I want to buy my gas at his house." Even Jeff Gordon joined the chorus, though he should know from experience that young drivers who win a bunch of races inevitably invite cries of CHEAT! (Remember the rumors back in '98 that Wonder Boy was treating his tires with some secret chemical formula?) As for Newman, he generally brushes off the controversy with a smile. "There's nothing wrong with grinning when you're winning," the driver says.

Expect to see plenty of Newman's pearly whites in 2004. Lost in all the talk about Newman's degree and alleged deviousness is the fact that the 26-year-old native of South Bend can drive the wheels off a race car. Already a member of the Quarter-Midget hall of fame, Newman has been pegged for the fast track ever since he won the All-American Midget Series championship in '93 at age 15. Owner Roger Penske put him in a stock car in '00, and Newman promptly won three ARCA races in a row. Newman led all Winston Cup drivers with 11 poles last season and now has 18 poles in 79 career races, which shows his ability to push his equipment to the limit. That fearlessness, combined with the obvious on-track smarts demonstrated by Newman and his crew, make the Alltel Dodge driver tough to beat. The allegations of cheating—does anyone think the NASCAR police wouldn't have caught Newman by now if he were playing fuel games—also show just how much the young driver has his competition spooked.

Newman's only glitch so far in a short but stellar career is an annual case of spring fever. After failing to finish four of the first 10 races last season, he found himself 27th in the standings last May 3. His rookie season started slowly as well, as he failed to finish three consecutive races (Texas, Martinsville and Talladega) out of the first 10. While the early struggles in 2002 could be attributed to rookie jitters, last season's switch to Dodge provided an explanation for another sluggish start. If Newman is going to win the first Nextel Cup, however, he can't dig such an immense hole before the weather warms up. Here's betting that the college guy figures it out. —*Pete McEntegart*

**RUNS WELL AT:** In two seasons Newman has nine victories on eight tracks, including two wins and four top 10s at Dover.

**TROUBLE SPOTS:** Newman must stay away from the Big One at restrictor-plate tracks. He has four DNFs in eight career starts at Daytona and Talladega, and three are due to wrecks.

**PROJECTION:** With Newman and Borland already showing uncanny chemistry and a mastery of on-track strategy, a championship for the number 12 team can't be too far away.

Fun Fact:
Newman got a big thrill out of meeting Dave Matthews after a concert in Charlotte in '03.

# 2

## Jeff GORDON

BEER CANS FLEW into the air. Strangers hugged. A few old ladies even whooped and hollered. Heading into Turn I of Lap I at the Sirius at the Glen last Aug. I0, the pole sitter, Jeff Gordon, was bumped from behind by rookie Greg Biffle, sending Gordon spinning out in a tornado of dust and prompting fans in the grandstand along the front straightaway to act as if they'd just won the lottery. It had been over a year since Gordon had heard a reaction like this, and although the noise was definitely not from fans cheering him on, it carried a sweet message nonetheless: After a season of disappointment, Gordon was back in the championship hunt.

"I know things aren't going well when the fans don't react to me," says Gordon. "So hearing the fans get excited about something that happens to me on the track means our team is doing something right."

Gordon finished 20th or worse in seven out of eight races in July and August, taking him out of contention for the points title, but consecutive wins at Martinsville and Atlanta in October and seven top fives in the last nine races gave him a fourth place finish in the final standings. The late-season surge means that the man who's captured four Winston Cup championships should be a serious threat to win the Nextel championship in '04. Why? Let Robbie Loomis, Gordon's crew chief, explain. "For the first time in a while there isn't a lot of turmoil in Jeff's personal life," says Loomis. "This year he's done a good job of blocking everything out and just focusing on racing, but it has to have an impact on your performance when things in your life aren't going well."

Adds Gordon, "I always said that I didn't let my divorce influence my driving, but in truth, it probably did. That's why I'm so excited for the future. It's all behind me now."

Gordon's very public divorce from wife Brooke was messy from the beginning. In the days leading up to last year's Daytona 500, for example, Brooke's lawyers scurried through the garage area handing out subpoenas to team owners such as Ray Evernham and Chip Ganassi in the hope of determining Gordon's net worth. The seven-and-a-half-year marriage between the Ken and Barbie of NASCAR ended last June, when Gordon reportedly agreed to give Brooke $15.3 million. Today Gordon doesn't like to even mention Brooke's name, preferring to focus on what's happening now in his life. In addition to the new apartment that he purchased in New York City early last year and his new girlfriend (model Amanda Church), Gordon has something even more important: a new outlook.

"I think I'm a little more relaxed now," says the 32-year-old Gordon. "It's taken a sense of humor to get through everything, so maybe I laugh a little bit more now as well."

Though Gordon has won only 15 races over the past four seasons—in 1998 alone he won 13—there's an air of quiet confidence emanating from Hendrick Motorsports as the 2004 season approaches. Gordon believes that in the midsummer months of the '03 schedule he experienced a year's worth of bad luck. Even when he did well in qualifying, as he did at Watkins Glen, something bad always seemed to happen. "You expect some bad breaks because that's just the nature of racing," says Gordon, "but hopefully all of ours are now out of the way. We think the future is bright."

If Gordon is right, the fans will certainly let him know. —*Lars Anderson*

---

**RUNS WELL AT:** Gordon has won more times at Darlington (six) than at any other venue, which is tops among active drivers.

**TROUBLE SPOTS:** Though he runs well on all types of tracks, the one venue Gordon has struggled at recently is Pocono, where his average finish in his last four starts has been 16th.

**PROJECTION:** Now that things have settled down in his personal life, Gordon will be looking to add a fifth points championship to his impressive racing résumé in 2004.

### Fun Fact:
Joe Montana, Michael Jordan and Tony Hawk are the athletes outside of racing whom Gordon most admires.

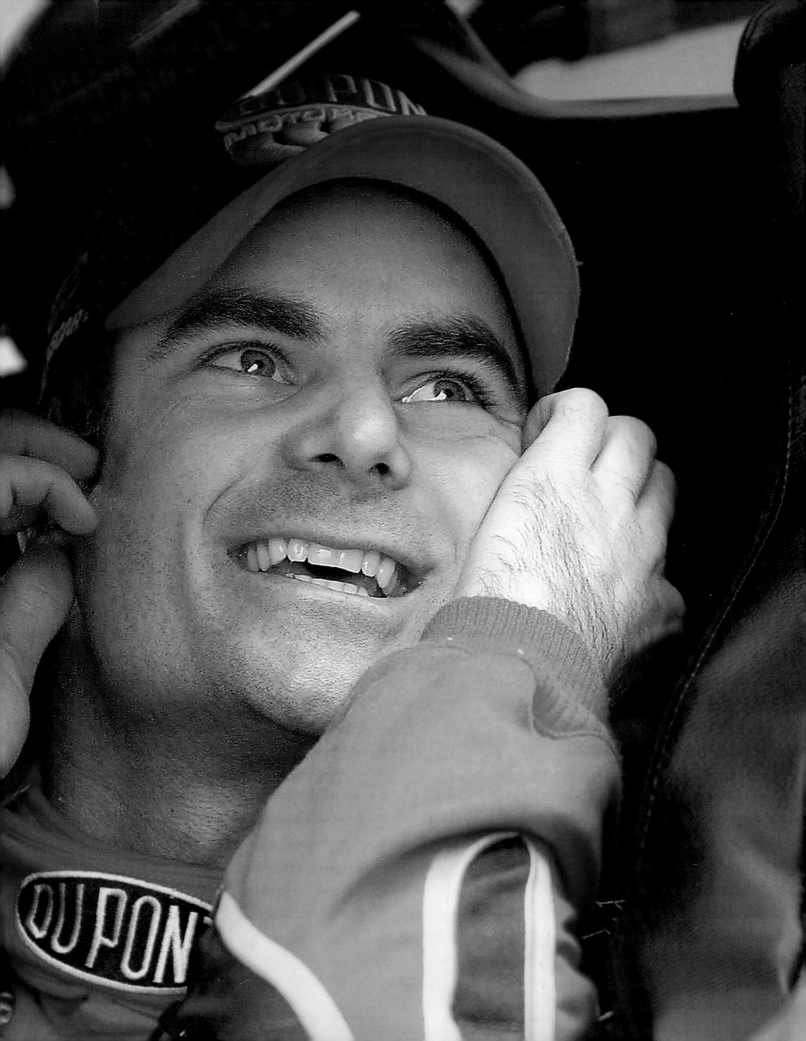

# 3
# Dale EARNHARDT Jr.

THEY CALL HIM the Franchise, a nickname Dale Earnhardt Jr.'s closest friends gave him after he purchased a boxing ring on the Internet last summer. Once Junior had assembled the ring in his garage—with his own two hands, he's proud to tell you—he and his friends would often spar, trading punches and laughs deep into the night. There was only one rule: no hitting the Franchise in the face.

"I'm giving up 40 pounds to most of my friends, so they only throw three-quarter punches," says Earnhardt, who is six feet tall and weighs 165 pounds. "The real reason I got it was because it helps me stay in shape. You couldn't pay me enough money to work out on a regular basis. But I love sparring, and it keeps me fit."

What's this? Dale Earnhardt talking about exercise? It's almost hard to believe, but Junior is 29 now, and he's starting to act his age. He no longer stays up late sucking on Budweisers with his friends in his basement-cum-watering hole known as Club E, and he no longer sleeps through interviews. Most important, though, he is no longer just Dale Sr.'s kid. As a physically fit Junior enters his fifth season on the NASCAR circuit, it's clear that he has become his own man.

"I was always under my dad's wing growing up," says Junior. "After his death I struggled to figure who I really was. But I feel like I've figured that out now."

Junior certainly forged his own identity on the track in 2003. He finished third in the points standings (his previous best was eighth, in '01) and he had a career-best 13 top five finishes. Always terrific on superspeedways—he's won four of the last five races at Talladega—last year Junior showed that he could also run well on intermediate and short tracks by winning at Phoenix in November and finishing third at Martinsville in April. In short he's rapidly developing into the kind of all-around driver who has the tools to win it all. "You can tell that Junior is gaining more confidence by the race," says Robbie Loomis, Jeff Gordon's crew chief. "He's clearly got the talent to win it all."

Matt Kenseth, who is one of Earnhardt's closest friends, agrees. "Next year I really think Junior is going to be in the middle of the race for the championship. He had some bad luck this year that put him behind a little, but by the end of the season he was running as good as anybody. His time is coming. You can just see it. I think most of the drivers feel that way."

Before the 2003 season Earnhardt overhauled his crew, with whom he had occasionally clashed in '02. The changes had the desired effect: The race team hummed throughout the '03 season. Junior gets along particularly well with his crew chief Tony Eury Sr., who is his uncle, and his car chief Tony Eury Jr., who is his cousin. Both Eurys have worked with the number 8 team since '99, and both are back for the '04 season. The one distraction the team faced in '03—Junior's uncertain contract situation with Dale Earnhardt Inc.—was resolved in October when Junior signed a five-year deal to remain at DEI.

"This team is close to being dominant," Junior says. "We've raced really well everywhere that we've been. The final part of the process is piling the results up." In other words, all the pieces are in place for Little E to become an even more intimidating presence in '04.          —L.A.

**RUNS WELL AT:** Junior has taken four of the last five checkered flags at Talladega, and he's a good bet to win at the Alabama superspeedway twice in 2004.

**TROUBLE SPOTS:** In his last four races at Dover, Junior's average finish is 26th. He won at the Monster Mile in '01, though, which means he has the potential to do well here in this season.

**PROJECTION:** If Junior can avoid finishing 30th or worse (which he did six times last season), he could be the Nextel champion.

**Fun Fact:** The guest room in Junior's house in Mooresville, N.C., is lined with pictures of Elvis Presley.

## 4 Jimmie JOHNSON

LAST SEASON: 4,932 POINTS, 2ND PLACE

THE TWO WOMEN seated behind Jimmie Johnson for Game 3 of the Lakers–Minnesota Timberwolves NBA playoff series in Los Angeles last April figured he must be *someone* because he was in the front row. As soon as Johnson took his seat courtside, the two started talking in a loud whisper. After a minute the blonde decided she had it figured out. "He's the Bachelor."

"No, he isn't," said the brunette.

"Yes, he is. I'll bet you a hundred dollars."

The blonde accepted and was ready to make it $200 when Johnson intervened. "I'm not the Bachelor," he said, producing his North Carolina driver's license as proof.

That, in a nutshell, was Jimmie Johnson's 2003 season: almost famous. After winning three races and finishing fifth in the points race as a rookie in 2002, he was poised for a breakout. But close calls and bad luck early in the season scuttled any championship hopes that he might have harbored.

It started at the Daytona 500, which Johnson would have won had the heavens opened 15 minutes before they did. Instead the rain held until Michael Waltrip worked his way past, leaving Johnson third. Then a couple of late-race scrapes with Sterling Marlin and a spinout on the last lap in Talladega turned great finishes into decent ones.

But Johnson rebounded, winning the Winston on May 17. After the race he and his crew chief, Chad Knaus, amazed owner Rick Hendrick with their conversation in the van en route to the press conference. Rather than whooping it up, said Hendrick, "they're talking about how to make the [Coca-Cola] 600 car better with shocks and springs." It paid off handsomely when they won that race as well, giving Johnson $1.3 million worth of oversized checks in one eight-day span. "These guys are an awesome combination," said Hendrick. "Two of the best I've ever had."

Coming from the man who paired Jeff Gordon with Ray Evernham, that's lofty praise. But Johnson and Knaus clearly mesh. Neither is a good ol' boy (Johnson is a California native, Knaus is from Illinois), and they are close in age (28 and 32) and demeanor (laid-back with an intense side, intense with a laid-back side). "I can look in his eyes and see what he's feeling," Knaus said, which would sound like absolute bunk were it not for the fact that the Johnson-Knaus partnership has been in the top 10 in points for 69 consecutive weeks, NASCAR's longest active streak. Johnson was also the only driver to stay in the top 10 wire to wire last year, which is impressive considering the season was largely a learning experience. "I've made some mistakes, had some failures, had some bad luck," said Johnson late in the season, "but I just feel so much further ahead as a driver, and the team is so much more mature."

Things should only get better for Johnson in his third season. He and Knaus signed extensions with Hendrick through 2007, insuring that Johnson won't have to worry about any distractions. And the moxie he showed after his rough start bodes well for a season in which the racing gods owe him a break or two. So it shouldn't be long before people start saying, Hey, the Bachelor looks like Jimmie Johnson. —*Mark Bechtel*

**RUNS WELL AT:** His car is sponsored by Lowe's, and Johnson does well at the track with the company name. In his last four races there, he hasn't finished worse than seventh and he won in 2003.

**TROUBLE SPOTS:** The only tracks where he has never finished in the top 10 are Richmond (in four races) and Sonoma (two races).

**PROJECTION:** This team might be NASCAR's best all-around operation, and with the driver, crew chief and sponsor locked up for four more years, there's no reason Johnson can't win it all.

**Fun Fact:** In 2000 Johnson was selected as one of PEOPLE magazine's "Sexiest Men in the Fast Lane."

THEY BOOED HIM during qualifying. Then they booed him even louder the next day when he was introduced before the Sharpie 500 at Bristol Motor Speedway. And after Kurt Busch won the race on Aug. 23, the fans booed so loudly that as Busch stood in Victory Lane, he could barely hear himself talk above the deafening disapproval thundering down from the 160,000 fans. Yet Busch was unfazed. Speaking into a microphone that was piped over the Speedway's P.A. system, Busch smiled smugly and said, "The late Dale [Earnhardt] Sr. once told me, 'The guy with the most noise wins.' "

Newell Rubbermaid, Busch's primary sponsor on the number 97 Ford, must never have gotten the memo that says any p.r.—even the bad variety—is good p.r. Within days of the Bristol race, company executives scolded their 25-year-old driver and announced they were setting up a mentoring program that would consist of media training and regularly scheduled meetings between Busch and veteran competitors to help the young driver become a better citizen of NASCAR Nation. Will it work? The answer should go a long way toward determining whether Busch challenges for his first championship in 2004.

"Kurt just has a really, really bad attitude," says Kevin Harvick, no stranger to controversy himself. "Sometimes he just spins people out, runs into them and drives like an idiot. But he can wheel a race car, there's no doubt about it."

To understand how Busch became NASCAR's newest villain, go back to Aug. 17 at Michigan International Raceway. After he and driver Jimmy Spencer bumped into each other during the Michigan 400, Busch radioed his crew and, not thinking anyone else was listening, said he had tried to "flatten [Spencer's] fender," which likely would have caused Spencer to lose control of his Dodge. After the race Spencer, while being dared by Busch to "do something," punched Busch in the nose as Busch sat in his car. Speaking to reporters later, Busch said he'd done nothing to provoke Spencer. But when Busch's in-car audiotape was released to the public, even some of his most ardent supporters turned on him.

"Things can really get blown out of proportion quickly, and I've learned that," says Busch. "It can happen if you don't mind your p's and q's. I've learned from those mistakes."

While nearly everyone in the NASCAR garage feels that Busch has a lot of growing up to do, his talent is undeniable. Though he slipped to 11th in the final standings in 2003, over the last two seasons the Las Vegas native has more wins (eight) than any other driver except Ryan Newman (nine). If Busch can clean up his act and take a few cues in the consistency department from teammate and Winston Cup points champ Matt Kenseth (Busch had 12 finishes of 25th or worse last season while Kenseth had just three), he has the tools to give Roush Racing its second-straight championship.

"Kurt is incredibly skilled," says team owner Jack Roush. "He's got great instincts on everything except maybe, on some occasions, the way he handles what goes on between his ears. But he's getting wiser on that."

That's a step in the right direction—one of several Busch will need to take in 2004 to turn the boos into cheers.                    —L.A.

**RUNS WELL AT:** Busch's never-back-down attitude serves him well at Bristol Motor Speedway, where he bumped and banged his way to Victory Lane twice last season.

**TROUBLE SPOT:** Maybe it's the pressure of racing in his hometown, but Busch hasn't run well at Las Vegas the past two years, finishing 20th in 2002 and 38th last season.

**PROJECTION:** If Busch can spend less time creating controversy and concentrate on driving, a Nextel championship is possible.

## Fun Fact:
Busch briefly pursued a career as a pharmacist, studying for 1½ years at the University of Arizona.

## Matt KENSETH

LAST SEASON: 5,022 POINTS, 1ST PLACE

WHAT WAS RUNNING through his mind? That's what all the scribes wanted to know about Matt Kenseth, who had just crashed on Lap 69 of the Kansas 400 on Oct. 5. It was a sparkling afternoon on the prairie, and Kenseth had been cruising down the backstretch when Michael Waltrip spun out in front of him. While trying to avoid Waltrip, Kenseth slowed, spun his Ford, skidded across the Kansas Speedway grass, then smashed the nose of his car against the inside concrete wall. Kenseth then drove to the garage for repairs, and while his crew worked on the car, the 31-year-old driver didn't bother to get out. He just sat at the wheel, stone-faced, looking forward.

Reporters quickly gathered around the number 17 Ford. Kenseth had blown an engine the previous week at Talladega and finished 33rd. Now that he was destined for another points-sapping finish, was he nervous that his points lead, which he'd held since the fourth race of the season, was slipping away? Was he about to blow an emotional gasket?

"I pretty much wasn't thinking anything," said Kenseth a few weeks later at Atlanta. "I was just sitting there. Everyone thought I was having deep thoughts, but I was just being me."

So now we know. The secret to Matt Kenseth is that, no matter the circumstances, the guy's temperament doesn't change. Even when he lost 177 points during that two-week stretch in late September and early October, Kenseth never panicked. Instead, he exuded a quiet confidence

**RUNS WELL AT:** Kenseth runs well at virtually every track on the schedule, but he particularly likes Texas Motor Speedway. He won there in 2002 and finished sixth after qualifying 17th last year.

**TROUBLE SPOTS:** If Kenseth is battling for the championship heading into the last race of the season, at Homestead, he's in trouble. He's finished 43rd and 40th in the last two races there.

**PROJECTION:** With crew chief Robbie Reiser returning, everything is in place for Kenseth to make a run at a second championship.

**Fun Fact** A die-hard Metallica fan, Kenseth named his cat Lars after the band's drummer Lars Ulrich.

that is quickly becoming his hallmark.

"To me the key to our season was the [UAW-GM Quality 500] in Charlotte after we lost all those points at Talladega and Kansas City," says Mike Calinoff, Kenseth's spotter, of the Oct. 11 race in which Kenseth finished eighth. "When we got to the track, Matt was joking around. He was confident. His attitude rubbed off on the entire team. That's the way it was all year long."

How good was Kenseth in 2003? He had 25 top 10 finishes and only three finishes of 30th or worse. "The thing about me is that I'm never satisfied," says Kenseth. "No one on our team ever is. That's why we never think any lead in a race, or in the points race, is safe. It's what keeps us sharp, and hopefully it will keep us in the championship hunt next season." —L.A.

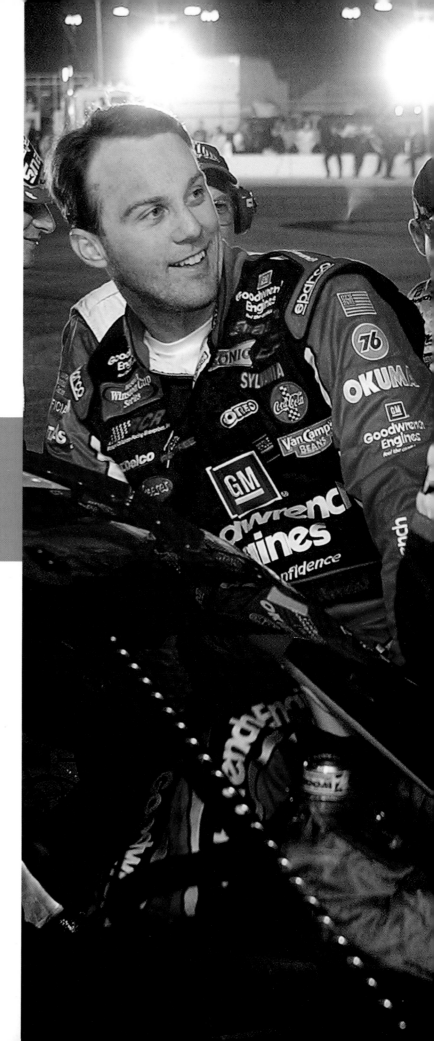

# 7

## Kevin HARVICK

**LAST SEASON:** 4,770 POINTS, 5TH PLACE

PINNING A PITHY description on Kevin Harvick is as treacherous as trying to keep him on your rear bumper. In 2001, when Harvick stepped into the impossible-to-fill fire suit of Dale Earnhardt and found Victory Lane in his third start, he was labeled the Can't Miss Kid. He won rookie of the year honors by finishing ninth in the Winston Cup standings while also winning the Busch title, and his youthful brashness was refreshingly reminiscent of the Man in Black. But in '02 Harvick became synonymous with *hothead*, as a series of fender-bending incidents and his all-around insolence led NASCAR to sit him down for a race, and he finished a mediocre 21st in the standings.

Turn the page to '03, when a strong midsummer run after nearly a year without major controversy led to a slew of HARVICK HAS MATURED headlines. Those were rewritten when Harvick and several of his crew members treated Ricky Rudd's car like a jungle gym after the Sept. 6 Richmond race. Harvick insisted that Rudd, who was battling him for the lead, had spun him out intentionally when Harvick was running second with

**RUNS WELL AT:** Harvick won the first two races ever run at Chicagoland Speedway's 1.5-mile tri-oval and was running second in 2003 when he ran out of gas with three laps to go.

**TROUBLE SPOTS:** The California native has never finished better than 25th in three starts at California Speedway's two-mile oval.

**PROJECTION:** Despite speculation that owner Richard Childress and his driver weren't getting along, Childress extended Harvick's contract through 2006. The added stability will only help Harvick.

**Fun Fact:** Harvick skipped his senior prom at Bakersfield's North High to compete in a late-model stock race.

eight laps to go. The stomping incident led to a $35,000 fine and Harvick's third probation in as many years. Not that Harvick lets probation cramp his hard-charging style. "You can do the things you always did," Harvick says. "You just can't go out of your territory."

After finishing fifth last season, Harvick has proven that his territory includes the top of the standings. The 28-year-old native of Bakersfield, who received a go-kart as a present for his kindergarten graduation, is as natural a driver as anyone on the circuit. More important, he has that rare quality of controlled aggression that's necessary to win a championship. Harvick isn't afraid to tangle with anyone for a victory.

Yet Harvick has learned how to play it safe. In '03 he finished every race, avoiding the big crash or blown engine that can derail a championship hunt. Since reuniting in March with crew chief Todd Berrier—who had piloted him to the Busch title in '01—Harvick has had 17 top 10 finishes in 31 races. He can also rely on the deep pockets of the Richard Childress Racing team, which helped Earnhardt to six of his seven titles. It shouldn't shock anyone if Harvick adds to that number and writes yet another headline.          —P.M.

# 8

## Tony STEWART

LAST SEASON: 4,549 POINTS, 7TH PLACE

TONY STEWART spent the first half of the 2003 season on his best behavior, which, alas, is not conducive to good racing. Without a major off-track incident to his credit, he floundered, and a string of three straight finishes of 40th or worse left him in 20th place heading into June. A happy Tony Stewart, it seems, is a slow Tony Stewart.

But in midsummer Stewart, who finished his '02 championship season on probation for serially surly behavior—including taking a swing at a photographer—reverted to his headline-grabbing ways. First was the courtship by owner Chip Ganassi. (Stewart re-signed with Joe Gibbs through '09 in August.) Then he ripped Goodyear after the fall Dover race, when he got what he felt was a subpar set of tires on his last pit stop. "They sponsor all these teams, and basically what it is, is hush money," Stewart said. "And I'm tired of covering their ass. I mean, it's pretty bad that the sets of tires are so bad that you can't make an adjustment on the car and go out and win the race when you've got the fastest car." He then told a television reporter who asked if the tires were different from earlier sets, "Ask Goodyear. They're the ones that built the pieces of s---." (Goodyear's Greg Stucker, general manager of marketing for stock car racing, said his company checked the tires, the production data on the tires and went over lap times from the Dover race and found nothing out of line with each individual set.)

Sufficiently miffed, Stewart then showed what he

**RUNS WELL AT:** No one seems to like to drive at New Hampshire, Phoenix and Homestead, but they're Stewart's bread-and-butter.

**TROUBLE SPOTS:** Daytona. If he's not flying through the air (the 2001 Daytona 500) or losing an engine three laps into the race (the '02 Daytona 500), he's usually running near the middle of the pack.

**PROJECTION:** No one has ever doubted Stewart's ability to drive, and the way he handled the 2002 season showed he can focus on racing when all hell is breaking loose.

### Fun Fact:
Stewart's favorite actress is Crystal Bernard, who played Helen Hackett on the sitcom *Wings*.

was capable of, winning at Lowe's Speedway the following week by erasing an eight-second deficit to Newman under green. "For once the fastest car wins the race!" Stewart said. "Hey, I've been trying to strike a blow for pure racing ever since I got here."

When it comes to pure racing, few are in Stewart's class. And his autumn rally to seventh place in the standings can't have his competitors feeling good about competing against him in '04. "Anytime you can finish the year as strong as we've been in the last three or four weeks, it's sure going to help [the following season]," said Greg Zipadelli, Stewart's crew chief.

Now if he can only figure out a way to get his driver angry earlier in the year. —*Mark Bechtel*

# 9

BOBBY LABONTE has a reputation for being as bland as grits with no butter or salt and pepper. Reporters scrambling for juicy postrace quotes steer clear of the taciturn Texan, who typically offers up such banalities as, "Sometimes you're on top, and sometimes you're on the bottom," or "I think I know some things, but I'm not going to talk about it." Such equanimity may not endear Labonte to the media, but it has generally been his ally on the track, especially during his 2000 championship season, when he avoided trouble so well that he finished every race (completing all but nine of 10,167 laps). But when Labonte placed 16th in the '02 points race—his worst performance since joining Joe Gibbs's team in '95—it was clear that consistency had dulled him into complacency.

Enter Michael (Fatback) McSwain. The tobacco-chewing, cuss-spewing, wrench-tossing crew chief from the mountains of North Carolina joined Labonte in October of last season, when longtime crew chief Jimmy Makar became general manager of Gibbs's two-car operation. For Labonte this change has been good,

**RUNS WELL AT:** Labonte closes nearly as well as Braves pitcher John Smoltz in Atlanta, winning a race at the Hampton, Ga., track in six of the past eight seasons.

**TROUBLE SPOTS:** The Daytona 500 has been a struggle for Labonte. He has a career average finish of 22.9 in 11 starts.

**PROJECTION:** Labonte and his sponsor, Interstate Batteries, are both signed with the well-oiled Gibbs operation through 2008, while McSwain has a deal through '06.

## Fun Fact:
Labonte tried but failed to book his favorite singer, Jimmy Buffett, for his championship banquet in 2000.

as was evident in the season's fourth race at Atlanta Motor Speedway, when Labonte responded to McSwain's constant encouragement by bumping Jeff Gordon out of the way with 11 laps to go and pulling away for the victory. "He is pretty calm, pretty conservative and kind of laid-back," says McSwain of his driver. "Have you seen the commercial with the little devil sitting on someone's shoulder? Well, that's me in his ear going, 'This is your race if you want it. Don't take nothing from these young kids.'"

Labonte was looking like a legitimate title contender through the midpoint of 2003, finishing in the top three in five straight races in one stretch. After taking fifth place at the Pepsi 400 on July 5, the number 18 car had 10 top fives, and Labonte was fourth in the standings through late July. He could certainly have used some of his famed consistency from that point on. Though he won the season's last race, at Homestead, Labonte had four DNFs (three engine failures and one accident) in a disappointing second half that left him eighth in the final standings. Even so, the laconic Labonte and the motormouth McSwain showed that opposites can combine for attractive results. Complacent no more, Labonte will once again be a contender in '04.   —P.M.

## 10

## Robby GORDON

LAST SEASON: 3,856 POINTS, 16TH PLACE

PUT ROBBY GORDON in any kind of car and chances are he'll drive it fast. Really fast. He's come within a whisker of winning the Indy 500 (he ran out of gas while leading on the last lap in 1999), he's won the Baja 1000 off-road race twice, and he's had a four-year winning streak in the 24 Hours of Daytona.

One thing he had never been able to do before 2003, however, was perform with consistency behind the wheel of a stock car. A big reason was his headstrong temperament, which consigned him to journeyman status. Before Richard Childress hired him full time late in 2001, Gordon had driven 52 races for nine teams in parts of eight seasons, torching the occasional bridge along the way.

Childress, though, made his name as an owner partnering with a notoriously uncongenial driver, Dale Earnhardt. After Childress gave Gordon the Intimidator's old crew, led by chief Kevin Hamlin, midway through the 2002 season, Gordon began to respond. In 2003 he made a strong run at a top 10 finish, faring especially well on the tracks where there's a premium on skill: road courses and flat tracks. He became only the second driver to sweep the two road races, taking the first, at Sonoma, in controversial fashion when he passed teammate Kevin Harvick racing back to a yellow flag—a violation of NASCAR's unwritten gentleman's agreement. That put him in the top 10, and he followed it up with a sixth-place finish at Michigan. But he wrecked in each of the next three races, the third while running near the front with 18 laps to go at Richmond. After Jeff Burton hit Gordon from behind, the new, calmer Gordon nearly had a relapse, seething over the radio, "He's getting a black eye. I'll pay my 25 grand [fine]."

That hollow threat was as close as Gordon came to

**RUNS WELL AT:** Tracks with right-hand turns. Gordon's average finish at Infineon Raceway and Watkins Glen International the past two seasons has been 4.0.

**TROUBLE SPOTS:** Atlanta. It's big and banked, two things Gordon doesn't like, and doesn't require much braking or shifting, two things he's good at. His best finish there has been 17th.

**PROJECTION:** Signed to a multiyear deal with RCR, Gordon is poised to have his best NASCAR season yet.

**Fun Fact:** Gordon has completed the Indy 500–Coca Cola 600 Memorial Day weekend double two times.

losing his cool in 2003. "I have had so many opportunities to be competitive, and I have let them slip away time and again," he said. "Now that I'm 34, I have learned from my past mistakes, and I'm a smarter driver." Even though the three wrecks crippled his mojo—Gordon limped home with nothing better than a 12th place finish in his last 13 races, dropping him from 10th to 16th in the standings—that newfound serenity plus another year spent in the RCR stable make Gordon a top 10 threat in 2004.  —*Mark Bechtel*

# 11

## Michael WALTRIP

LAST SEASON: 3,934 POINTS, 15TH PLACE

HAS ANY driver been granted respect more grudgingly than Michael Waltrip? Darrell's little brother was derided as Mr. 0-for-462 before his breakthrough win at the 2001 Daytona 500, but sadly that race will always be better remembered as the last one for Waltrip's car owner, Dale Earnhardt. When Waltrip added victories at the '02 Pepsi 400 and a rain-shortened '03 Daytona 500, critics asked when he would win at a track other than NASCAR's most hallowed ground. Then Waltrip held off teammate Dale Earnhardt Jr. to win at Talladega on Sept. 28 and the nabobs nattered about his inability to win anywhere but Daytona and Talladega, the only tracks where cars are fitted with horsepower-sapping restrictor plates. "For a long time I was told I couldn't do anything right," says the ever-cheerful Waltrip, 40. "Now they say I only do restrictor-plate races right. At least I've got that going for me."

These days Waltrip has many more

**RUNS WELL AT:** Surprise!—Daytona and Talladega. Since joining DEI before the 2001 season, Waltrip has four wins and eight top 10s in 12 starts at these tracks.

**TROUBLE SPOTS:** Since 2001, Waltrip has no top 10s and an average finish of 26th at Bristol, Martinsville and Richmond.

**PROJECTION:** Backed by DEI's exceptional equipment, a more confident Waltrip should find himself solidly in the top 10 for the first time in his 19-year career.

## Fun Fact: At 6'5" Waltrip is the tallest Nextel Cup driver. He has also run three marathons, the fastest in 4:16.

reasons to be optimistic. Buoyed by a strong relationship with crew chief Richard (Slugger) Labbe—who came aboard late in the '01 season in which Waltrip finished 24th—and a renewed commitment to fitness that keeps him fresh late in races, Waltrip is no longer just a drafting specialist. His seven top fives in '03 included third- and fifth-place finishes at the intermediate-length tracks Las Vegas and Darlington, respectively, and he finished 13th and ninth the past two years at Watkins Glen.

Waltrip's next hurdle will be keeping it together for a whole season. Last year he was a fixture in the top 10 through mid-September, but five DNFs in a 10-race span dropped him to 15th place in the final standings. If Waltrip can demonstrate his newfound versatility more often, he just might get some credit yet. —P.M.

# 12

## Jamie McMURRAY

LAST SEASON: 3,965 POINTS, 13TH PLACE

THOUGH HE never made it to Victory Lane in '03, Jamie McMurray proved that his surprising win at Charlotte on Oct. 13, 2002, was no fluke. In that race (only his second career start) he benefited from the fast car and accomplished crew of Sterling Marlin, whom McMurray replaced after Marlin fractured a vertebra in his neck in a wreck at Kansas City on Sept. 29. In 2003 owner Chip Ganassi more or less forced the 27-year-old native of Joplin, Mo., to make it on his own, outfitting McMurray (technically still a rookie because he had completed fewer than eight races) with an entirely new crew, led by veteran crew chief Donnie Wingo. "Not only is it tough to try to win a race, but also we have to try to do it with a brand-new team," McMurray said last spring.

That brand-new team got off to a rough start, blowing engines at Atlanta in March and Martinsville in April and bungling a pit stop at Dover in June. "It's been pretty frustrating," said McMurray at the time. "We just have to iron everything out." The wrinkles, indeed, began to disappear in the second half of the season, as McMurray and his team got to race on several tracks for a second time. As low as 30th in the standings in April, McMurray began a steady climb up the points list. Boosted by 12 finishes in the

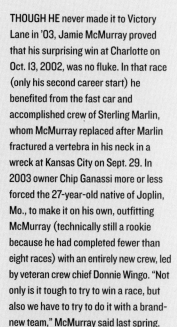

**RUNS WELL AT:** Though he got his first Winston Cup win at Charlotte, McMurray shone last year at Bristol, where he finished 11th in the Food City 500 and third in the Sharpie 500.

**TROUBLE SPOTS:** Two of McMurray's worst performances of 2003 came at Daytona, where he finished 31st and 37th.

**PROJECTION:** With a year of experience under his tires, McMurray stands on the cusp of NASCAR's elite. He's a good bet to get his second career win this season and may even crack the top 10.

## Fun Fact: McMurray began racing go-karts at age eight and won four U.S. go-kart titles between 1986 and '92.

top 10, including third-place runs at Indianapolis and Bristol, he finished the season in 13th place in the standings, and won the Raybestos Rookie of the Year award in a walk.

Now all he needs is a victory. "I knew coming into the season that realistically, with a new team, we probably weren't going to win our first or second race out," says McMurray. "I knew it would take a little time for our team to build. So I'm really looking forward to next year." —Mark Beech

# 13

## RustyWALLACE

LAST SEASON: 3,950 POINTS, 14TH PLACE

WITH A 71-race winless slump weighing heavily on his shoulders, Rusty Wallace was closing in on his first victory in two seasons at the Auto Club 500 at California Speedway last April. His number 2 Miller Lite Dodge had been dominant all afternoon, and Wallace was in front with 12 laps left. Then Kurt Busch dived low in Turn 3, pushed ahead and went on to win his second race—sending Wallace home with his losing streak intact. "I never saw him coming," Wallace said afterward. "There was a big drag race coming out of Turn four, and he beat me by six inches."

That finish was indicative of Wallace's terrible 2003 season. Although his driving ability and a car he described as "an incredible hot rod" led him to 12 top 10 finishes, Wallace failed to take the checkered flag for the second consecutive year, and his unhappiness showed.

After a poorly timed pit stop at the

**RUNS WELL AT:** Wallace dominates at short tracks, especially Bristol, where he has won nine races and seven poles.

**TROUBLE SPOTS:** Only four points champions—Bobby Isaac, Alan Kulwicki, Tony Stewart and Wallace—have never won at Darlington.

**PROJECTION:** Wallace's negative comments about his team raised the possibility that crew chief Bill Wilburn might be fired, but Wallace and team owner Roger Penske are hoping that keeping the team together will translate into better results in '04.

**Fun Fact:** In Newton, Iowa, Wallace has become the first driver to design a track anywhere. It should open in November.

Pennsylvania 500 on July 27 kept him lagging in 11th position, Wallace ripped into his crew, saying, "I love my team, there's no doubt, but when they make a mistake they have to take responsibility. We've lost many races with some bad pit calls, so my comment that, 'When I come down pit road, it scares me to death,' is something I'm not backing off on."

A streak of bad luck in August, which included a brake problem at Watkins Glen and early crashes at both Bristol and Darlington, helped ensure that Wallace would end the season out of the top 10 for the first time since 1992. If the 47-year-old Wallace, who has 54 career wins, is to get back to the top of the standings in '04, he'll first need to make a return visit to a place he hasn't seen since April 29, 2001: Victory Lane. —*Andrea Woo*

# 14

## SterlingMARLIN

LAST SEASON: 3,745 POINTS, 18TH PLACE

ON SEPT. 29, 2002, Sterling Marlin was nearing the end of the best season of his 27-year career. The 46-year-old driver had led the points standings for 25 weeks and was only seven good finishes from his first Winston Cup championship when Jeff Burton clipped him from behind on Lap 148 at Kansas Speedway and sent him into the wall. Marlin not only suffered a cracked vertebra in his neck, sidelining him for the rest of the season, but also the accident marked the beginning of a streak of bad luck that continued throughout '03.

Marlin, who has 10 wins in his career, had more than his share of setbacks last season. He received a controversial black flag at Daytona for driving below the yellow line, blew his water pump at Rockingham, got caught behind a wreck at Darlington and led 157 laps at the Sirius 400 at Michigan in June before a missed a gear on a late restart dropped him back to a sixth-place finish. Each race added to the frustration.

"We've had a top five car probably eight or 10 times and just haven't capitalized on it," Marlin said in October. "We've lost a couple of motors, and I've been caught in four or five wrecks that weren't our fault. It's just rotten, rotten luck." He ended the year without a top

**RUNS WELL AT:** Restrictor plate tracks: Since 1990 Marlin has 10 top five finishes (including three wins) and four poles at Daytona. He also has two wins and three poles at Talladega.

**TROUBLE SPOTS:** Marlin has had little success at Watkins Glen International over the last five years, finishing no better than 25th.

**PROJECTION:** The number 40 Coors Light team, led by crew chief Lee McCall, remains basically intact, but stability will not necessarily lead to better results for Marlin in 2004.

**Fun Fact:** Marlin was the captain of the Spring Hill (Tenn.) High football team in 1975, playing quarterback and linebacker.

five finish and ranked 18th in points.

Will Marlin's luck change in 2004? Tony Glover, Marlin's team manager, thinks he has a good chance. "When you get momentum going, you get a lot of confidence and a lot of positive energy, and it's not that difficult then to have good runs," he says. "But when things start going wrong, each week it seems like it gets a little harder on everyone involved. A good team can rebound from this, and we've got to show we're a class race team."—A.W.

# 15

## Jeff BURTON
LAST SEASON: 4,109 POINTS, 12TH PLACE

WHILE ROUSH Racing teammate Matt Kenseth was cruising toward a Winston Cup points championship, 36-year-old Jeff Burton found himself out of the top 10 for the second straight year despite completely overhauling his number 99 team.

The changes began in September 2002, when crew chief Frank Stoddard, who had won 14 races with Burton between '98 and '01, was replaced with Paul Andrews (who had teamed with the late Alan Kulwicki to win the '92 points championship). The makeover continued in the off-season, and Burton started last year with only five crew members remaining from the previous season.

Perhaps the biggest adjustment was made by Burton himself. The old school driver from South Boston, Va., had been accustomed to making all the decisions about springs, shocks and front-end setups, but he finally decided to turn over this responsibility

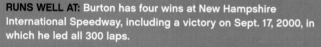

**RUNS WELL AT:** Burton has four wins at New Hampshire International Speedway, including a victory on Sept. 17, 2000, in which he led all 300 laps.

**TROUBLE SPOTS:** Burton did not fare well on road courses last season, finishing 38th at Sonoma and 31st at Watkins Glen.

**PROJECTION:** Roush signed Burton to a multiyear deal in September, but the number 99 team was still searching for a primary sponsor at press time.

**Fun Fact:** Burton hosts a fishing tournament in Lake Buena Vista, Fla., to raise money for the Muscular Dystrophy Association.

to his crew. "Drivers need to be willing to step back and say, I'm not smart enough nor do I have enough time to understand everything from an engineering standpoint," Burton says. "There's so much more technology today, so many different ways of looking at things."

The changes his team has made have been slow to pay off, as Burton managed just three top five finishes last season, at Martinsville, Daytona and Richmond. But he sees no reason to be discouraged heading into the 2004 season. "I see us building," Burton says. "If you were just an outsider looking in and you just looked at the finishes, you'd say, 'They're no better than they were.' But I know that we've made a huge improvement and I know that we've put ourselves in contention to win."

—Julia Morrill

# 16

## Terry LABONTE
LAST SEASON: 4,162, 10TH PLACE

WITH THE performance he gave on the track in 2003, Terry Labonte was the natural choice for the *TSN* Comeback Driver of the Year award. Coming off disappointing '01 and '02 campaigns in which he finished 23rd and 24th, respectively, Labonte enjoyed a major resurgence last season, finishing 10th in the Winston Cup point standings.

The highlight of the season, for Labonte and his fans, was the 46-year-old former two-time Winston Cup champion's victory at Darlington Raceway, in the last Southern 500 to be held on Labor Day weekend. The win broke a 156-race winless streak, something that might have prompted over-the-top celebrations by some drivers but only inspired the mild-mannered Labonte to drive calmly to Victory Lane while the crowd of 65,000 stood and cheered. Despite his response—Labonte told fans he was "too old to do donuts"—the win meant plenty to the stoic Texan. "Darlington has always been a special place to me just because of the fact that I won my first race there," he said. "To win the final one was pretty special."

The roots of Labonte's revival can be traced to the spring of 2002, when car owner Rick Hendrick promoted chief mechanic Jim Long to crew chief for Labonte's number 5 team. Long brought

**RUNS WELL AT:** The oval track at Richmond suits Labonte's racing style. He has finished in the top ten in 27 of 51 races there.

**TROUBLE SPOTS:** Labonte struggles at New Hampshire. In his previous 10 races at Loudon, his average finish is 25th —including a 43rd at the July 2000 race.

**PROJECTION:** Labonte's '03 performance helped him keep his ride, but he'll need another strong showing in '04 to keep 18-year-old Kyle Busch from taking Labonte's seat in the number 5 Chevy.

**Fun Fact:** A life-sized replica of Terry Labonte's car, sculpted out of 3,500 pounds of cheese was on display at Richmond in May.

in new body styles after testing the cars in the wind tunnel, something previous crew chief Gary DeHart wasn't fond of doing. This helped Labonte's Chevrolet's run more consistently from week to week. "It took a while to figure out what to do and for me and the team to get used to each other," says Long. Last season the team seemed to be clicking. What's more, Labonte's Southern 500 win sent a message to the rest of the field: His career is far from over, even after 25 years on the circuit. —J.M.

## 17

### Mark MARTIN
LAST SEASON: 3,769 POINTS, 17TH PLACE

LAST SEASON Mark Martin finally got his name on a Winston Cup trophy, but it didn't happen the way he had always imagined. When Matt Kenseth clinched the 2003 points championship in Rockingham, standing beside him was Martin, his teammate and the number 17 car's co-owner.

The 44-year-old Martin—who had brought Kenseth to the attention of car owner Jack Roush, essentially launching the youngster from the short tracks of Wisconsin to a title at his sport's highest level—called the moment bittersweet and even hinted that it might be time for him to retire. After all, Martin was wrapping up a 17th-place finish in the point standings and was riding a 60-race winless streak, the second longest of his career since joining Roush Racing in 1988. Although he had finished among the top three in the points race eight times in his 22-year career, maybe it was time to pass the torch for good.

**RUNS WELL AT:** Martin's favorite track is the 1.5 mile Lowe's Motor Speedway, the site of his last win, the Coca Cola 600, in May 2002. Martin also has seven wins at Bristol Motor Speedway.

**TROUBLE SPOTS:** Martin has three career wins at Dover International Speedway, but none since the 1999 season.

**PROJECTION:** Coming off his worst season since joining the Roush Racing team in 1988, Martin hopes the switch to new crew chief Pat Tryson will change his luck in 2004.

**Fun Fact:** In 2003 Martin's 11-year-old son Matt became the youngest driver ever to be signed by Ford.

The gloom didn't last, however. In early November, Martin—a Viagra spokesman, after all—took a step toward rejuvenating his career when his team made a key personnel change. On Nov. 2 Roush Racing and the Wood Brothers teams switched crew chiefs, with Pat Tryson replacing Ben Leslie in Martin's garage. "We've made similar changes with chemistry in the past, and it has been very effective," Roush said. A shake-up had helped Martin once before; he finished the 2001 season in 12th place, then, after Leslie replaced crew chief Jimmy Fennig, Martin drove his Ford to within 38 points of the 2002 Winston Cup championship. While hopes are high, it's not likely that a simple change will be enough to enable Martin to finally hoist a Nextel Series trophy all his own.          —J.M.

## 18

### Ward BURTON
LAST SEASON: 3,550, 21ST PLACE

AFTER STRUGGLING through one of the worst stretches of his 10-year career, Ward Burton is starting over with a new car, a new owner and a new outlook. Last season, citing a "lack of respect and lack of communication" between himself and longtime owner Bill Davis, Burton signed on to drive Gene Haas's No. 0 NetZero HiSpeed Pontiac. The first-year team struggled in 2003, scoring no top 10 finishes among four drivers (including Burton for the last four starts), but Burton had been intrigued enough by Haas's partnership with powerful Hendrick Motorsports to choose the team from among a handful of suitors. "This looked like the team that wanted me the most, and a team with the best opportunity for growth," he says. "This is a great opportunity for me to bring my experience to an up-and-coming young team."

New crew chief Tony Furr will be working to get consistency from Burton, whose uneven efforts were no doubt a factor in Davis's letting the driver out of the final season of his contract. In eight years with Davis, Burton finished in the top 10 of the point standings twice and won five races, including the 2002 Daytona 500. Mixed in with the wins, however, were far too many back-of-the-pack finishes. By the time he won at Daytona, Burton had begun a

**RUNS WELL AT:** Burton's old number 22 Caterpillar Dodge could always be counted on at restrictor plate events, and he has a victory in the Daytona 500 to prove it.

**TROUBLE SPOTS:** In the past seven years Burton has won the pole twice at Michigan International Speedway, but he has also finished 20th or worse there eight times.

**PROJECTION:** For all his experience, Burton is entering the season with a new crew and a new car. Expect him to struggle.

**Fun Fact:** Burton is one of only nine drivers to have won both the Daytona 500 and Darlington's Southern 500.

precipitous decline, finishing 25th in the points two years ago, and 21st last season—with no wins. "The average age of the winning drivers this year is 32," Davis said shortly before he and Burton, who turned 42 in October, split. "The average age of the top 10 in points is 30. That says it all."

Only time will tell if Burton is indeed over the hill. But a fresh start and a young team could go a long way toward helping him get back to the winner's circle in 2004.          —Mark Beech

## 19

## Brian VICKERS

LAST SEASON: BUSCH SERIES CHAMPION

SOMETIMES PARENTS can learn a lot from their kids. After a 2002 crash ended Ricky Hendrick's driving career when he was only 22, he decided to follow in the footsteps of his father, Rick, and become an owner. The first driver he wanted to hire, for the seat in the number 5 Busch car he had just vacated, was 19-year-old Brian Vickers. Alas, Hendrick's dad—also known as the guy with the checkbook—wasn't keen on the idea. "I pretty much told [my father] that these were my cars and my deal, and if he wanted me to be a part of it, then this was what I wanted to do," Ricky said. "Either I was going to get written out of the will and written out of my job, or he was going to go with it. And he went with it."

Vickers repaid Ricky's confidence in him and won Rick over by taking the Busch title in 2003. He did so in such impressive fashion (he won three times and had 21 top 10 finishes) that when Rick needed to fill the seat in the 25 car,

**RUNS WELL AT:** Vickers's Busch Series wins all came on challenging tracks with personality: Indianapolis Raceway Park, Darlington Raceway and Dover International Speedway.

**TROUBLE SPOTS:** He didn't fare so well at the cookie cutters: Kansas (32nd), Atlanta (31st), California (19th) and Texas (25th).

**PROJECTION:** Can Vickers handle the weight of the expectations being placed on his young shoulders? Every indication is he can, and he should run away with rookie of the year honors.

## Fun Fact:

By winning the Busch title last year at age 20, Vickers became the youngest NASCAR series champion.

which Joe Nemechek drove in the Winston Cup in '03, he did what his son did a year earlier: He picked Vickers.

A personable kid whose tastes vary from *Dumb and Dumber* to *The Count of Monte Cristo*, Vickers should thrive in the Hendrick phenom factory, which has churned out photogenic leadfoots Jeff Gordon and Jimmie Johnson. In a four-race stint with the team at the end of 2003, Vickers showed he and crew chief Peter Sospenzo could find the fast way around a track, never starting worse than fourth. His race finishes were not nearly as impressive (his average was 29.4), perhaps foreshadowing the pitfalls he'll face in '04: He's had little time with his current team, and he's driving against tougher competition than he's ever faced. Of course, he faced the same obstacles in '03, and things turned out pretty well. —*Mark Bechtel*

## 20

## Greg BIFFLE

LAST SEASON: 3,696 POINTS, 20TH PLACE

AFTER FIVE successful years in NASCAR's bush leagues, Greg Biffle made the jump to the Winston Cup Series in 2003 and found that he still had a lot to learn. The only driver to win championships—as well as rookie of the year awards—on both the Craftsmen Truck and Busch circuits, he and his crew struggled to build competitive cars at the highest level. Although he surprised observers by winning the Pepsi 400 at Daytona, Biffle raced to only six top 10 finishes this past season, the fewest of any driver in the top 20 of the point standings. "In the truck and Busch series the budgets aren't nearly as big and you don't go to the wind tunnel that much," he says. "It is more on the driver and crew back there."

If Biffle's problem was the way his car was running, he should see a difference this season. Last August, at the driver's insistence, team owner Jack Roush hired gaskets-and-gears man Doug Richert as crew chief, replacing Randy Goss, who had been with Biffle since 1998. The change appeared to pay off almost immediately as Biffle took two top 10 finishes in his first month with Richert.

Biffle said in June that he and his crew often felt like the fifth of five teams in the powerful Roush Racing

**RUNS WELL AT:** For all his inconsistency last year (he finished outside the top 20 16 times), Biffle was remarkably solid at Darlington, where he ran 12th and 10th in the two races.

**TROUBLE SPOTS:** Biffle says Pocono reminds him of the tight course at nearby Nazareth Speedway, where he has three wins; but he finished 20th and 27th at the Pennsylvania track in '03.

**PROJECTION:** Look for Biffle to improve this season under the guidance of new crew chief Doug Richert.

**Fun Fact:** At the Pepsi 400 in July, Biffle became the first rookie to win at Daytona since Mario Andretti in 1967.

stable, which also included established drivers Matt Kenseth, Kurt Busch, Jeff Burton and Mark Martin. In fact, Roush admitted that he had been "holding Greg back because our team wasn't strong enough" and was "spread too thin to lend in-house support."

If crew chief Richert can help the second-year driver get his car revved up this year, though, Biffle could find himself moving up in the team pecking order, as well as in the Nextel Cup standings. —*Mark Beech*

# The Track

## 2004 SCOUTING REPORTS

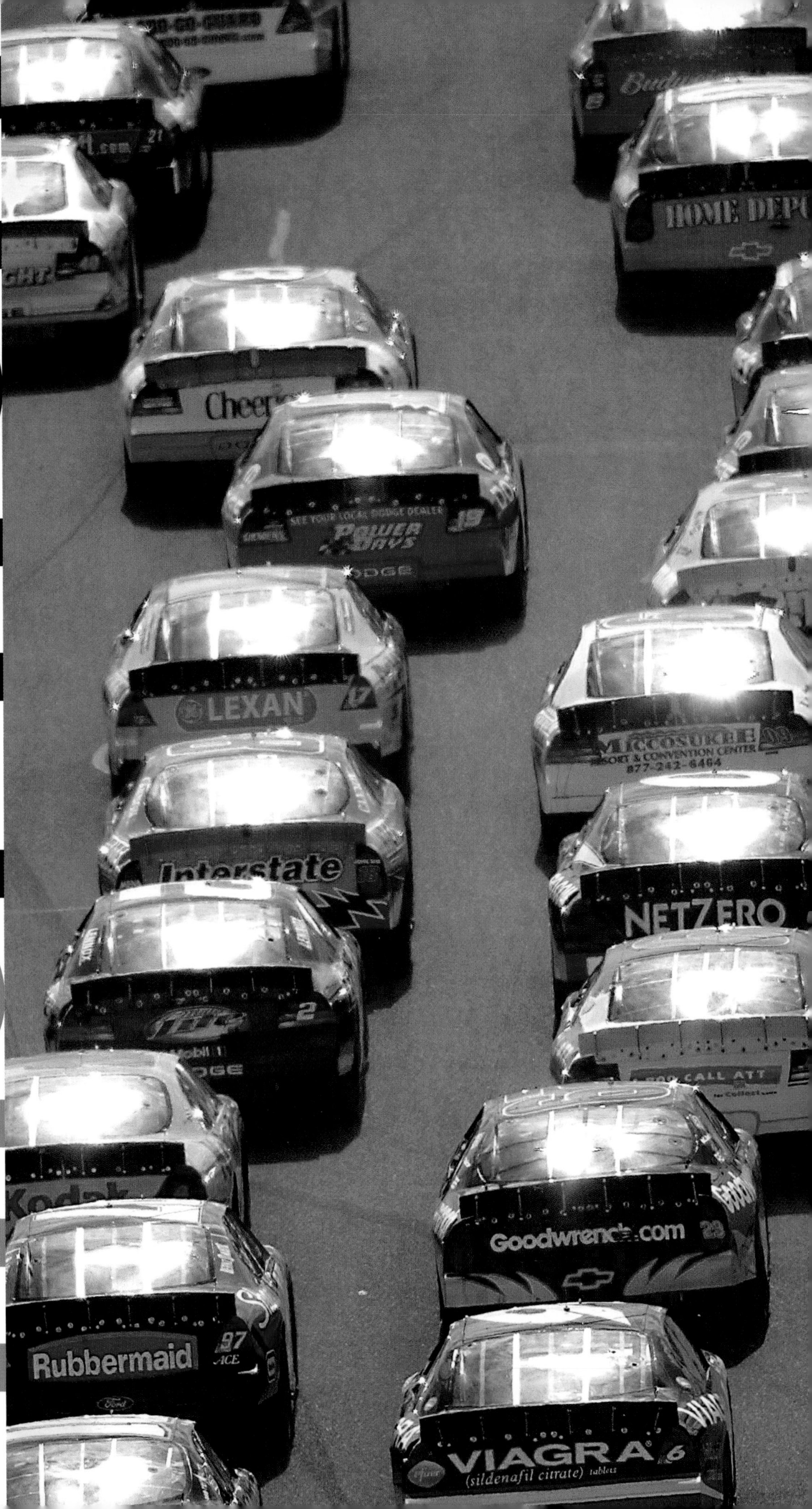

Scott WIMMER  Bill ELLIOTT  Dale JARRETT  Boris SAID

# Rookies to Watch

**BRENDAN GAUGHAN**   no. 77 Dodge   The Las Vegas–based driver had six Craftsman Truck Series victories in '03 and narrowly missed winning the points title. At press time he was the preferred candidate to take over for Dave Blaney.

**KASEY KAHNE**   no. 9 Dodge   One of the most coveted young drivers, Kahne will take over for Bill Elliott. He won the final Busch race of '03, and it wouldn't be a surprise if he got a victory in the Nextel Cup.

**SCOTT RIGGS**   no. 10 Chevrolet   The 32-year-old Riggs, who won four Busch races last year, finally gets his chance at NASCAR's highest level. He replaces Johnny Benson and is a dark-horse candidate for rookie of the year.

**JOHNNY SAUTER**   no. 30 Chevrolet   With an eighth place finish, the 25-year-old Wisconsin native helped Richard Childress claim the 2003 Busch Series owner's championship and his effort was rewarded with a promotion to Nextel Cup.

**SCOTT WIMMER**   no. 22 Dodge   Wimmer, who had one top 10 finish in six starts last season, takes over the 22 car, which had been driven by Ward Burton for the previous nine seasons. The 28-year-old driver has the tools to be a surprise winner in '04.

# Other Drivers

**JOHNNY BENSON**   team unknown   The 40-year-old Benson didn't have many memorable moments in '03. He did register two top fives and had a car fast enough to win at Homestead, but he was still searching for a ride at press time.

**TODD BODINE**   no. 54 Ford   Known for occasionally being too aggressive on the track, Bodine was knocked out of eight races (23% of his starts) by accidents in '03. Will his foot get lighter this season? Don't count on it.

**DERRIKE COPE**   no. 37 Chevrolet   Cope had a special talent in '03: He could blow up an engine faster than any other driver. Cope started 18 races last year and only finished five, with his best run coming at Las Vegas (29th).

**RICKY CRAVEN**   no. 32 Chevrolet   Last year Craven was the lowest-ranked driver in the point standings (27th) to win a race. He might get lucky on a setup and win again in '04, but his destiny appears to be that of a middle-of-the-pack driver.

**BILL ELLIOTT**   no. 91 Dodge   The 48-year-old decided it was time to scale back. He will try to run 15 races, starting with Las Vegas, if he can put together a sponsorship package. Elliott also plans to mentor his Evernham Motorsports teammates.

**JEFF GREEN**   no. 43 Dodge   Don't be fooled by the fact that Green had no top 10s in 31 starts in '03. This guy has talent, and the move to Petty Enterprises gives him a good chance to earn a Top 10 in '04.

**DALE JARRETT**   no. 88 Ford   Driving the UPS Ford, Jarrett didn't deliver the goods in '03. Jarrett finished 26th in points, but still has the support of owner Robert Yates, who signed Jarrett to a three-year contract extension in October.

**JEREMY MAYFIELD**   no. 19 Dodge   Mayfield finished last season as one of NASCAR's hottest drivers, chalking up four top fives in the last 11 races. He re-signed with Ray Evernham late in '03 and could emerge as a top-tier driver in '04.

**JOE NEMECHEK**   no. 01 Chevrolet   Nemechek was hired to drive for Richard Childress Racing while Jerry Nadeau continues to recover from an accident suffered at Richmond on May 2. Nemechek finished 10th in Atlanta in his first race in the U.S. Army car.

**KYLE PETTY**   no. 45 Dodge   One of the most likable drivers in the sport, Petty has only one top 10 in his last 60 starts. Last season he failed to qualify for three races and had an average finish of 29.9, numbers that hardly inspire comparisons with the King.

**TONY RAINES**   no. 74 Chevrolet   You have to admire Raines. Running without a primary sponsor all season in '03, he completed 9,152 of 10,508 laps and finished sixth at Rockingham in the fall. Still, he's a long shot to nab even a single top five in '04.

**RICKY RUDD**   no. 21 Ford   The 47-year-old Rudd showed spunk when he tangled with Kevin Harvick at the September Richmond race, but after finishing the season 19th in points, his best days appear to be behind him.

**ELLIOTT SADLER**   no. 38 Ford   Sadler had more bad luck than perhaps any other driver in '03 and he frequently seemed to get caught up in wrecks that weren't his fault. Expect him to improve dramatically over his 27th place finish.

**KEN SCHRADER**   no. 49 Dodge   The 48-year-old Schrader hasn't finished higher than 30th in the point standings in 10 years. But his two top 10s in '03 (Martinsville and Michigan) offer a glimmer of hope for '04.

**JIMMY SPENCER**   no. 7 Dodge   Mr. Excitement lost his primary sponsor—Sirius—at the end of '03, but his car owner Jim Smith says Spencer will run a full schedule in '04 even if they don't find a new sponsor.

# Road Course Specialists

**RON FELLOWS**   A 17-year road racing veteran, Fellows will once again compete only on the two road courses in '04. In 10 starts at Infineon Raceway and Watkins Glen International, the Mississauga, Ont., native's average finish is 30.8.

**BORIS SAID**   Said, another road course ringer, is especially dangerous at Infineon, where last year he won the pole and finished sixth. Said would like to find a full-time Nextel Cup ride in '05, and a win this season would go a long way toward making that happen.

# 2003
## THE SEASON IN PICTURES

It was definitely a beautiful year for NASCAR champion Matt Kenseth, who built a huge lead early, then stayed the course to capture his first points title

**PHOTOGRAPH BY ROBERT LABERGE/GETTY IMAGES**

**EASY DRIVER** MATT KENSETH COULD SAVOR THE SOUTH FLORIDA SCENERY ON THE FINAL STOP OF '03—HE'D CLINCHED THE TITLE THE PREVIOUS WEEK.

## 2.16 DAYTONA 500

DAYTONA INTERNATIONAL SPEEDWAY
**WINNER:** MICHAEL WALTRIP

Waltrip (lead car) got aerodynamic help from teammate Dale Earnhardt Jr. on the race's key restart but a bigger assist from Mother Nature as rain turned the 500 into a 272½.

**PHOTOGRAPH BY FRED VUICH**

## 2.23 SUBWAY 400

NORTH CAROLINA SPEEDWAY
**WINNER:** DALE JARRETT

Jarrett's tires had enough bite to hold off Kurt Busch at Rockingham as the pair traded the lead three times in the final 10 laps. Said Busch, "If the fans didn't dig that, they need help."

**PHOTOGRAPH BY NIGEL KINRADE**

## 3.02 UAW DAIMLER-CHRYSLER 400

LAS VEGAS MOTOR SPEEDWAY
**WINNER:** MATT KENSETH

Kenseth took his only checkered flag of the season thanks to some fine pit stops—including a four-tire change in a blistering 13 seconds—and one he mistakenly, and fortuitously, skipped on Lap 138.

**PHOTOGRAPH BY GARY SOLOMONS/ASP INC.**

## 3.09 BASS PRO SHOPS MBNA 500

ATLANTA MOTOR SPEEDWAY
**WINNER:** BOBBY LABONTE

The number 18 and 24 cars got even closer than this with 11 laps to go when Labonte (18) bumped Gordon aside for the lead en route to his sixth career victory at Atlanta and his first in a Chevy.

**PHOTOGRAPH BY GEORGE TIEDEMANN/GT IMAGES**

**GRASS LANDING**
RYAN NEWMAN WAS UNHURT IN THIS DAYTONA TUMBLE, BUT WOUND UP WITH A TWO-FOOT CHUNK OF SOD IN HIS LAP.

PHOTOGRAPH BY
F. PEIRCE WILLIAMS/ASP INC.

# 3.16 CAROLINA DODGE DEALERS 400

DARLINGTON RACEWAY
**WINNER: RICKY CRAVEN**

After Craven (32) and Kurt Busch rubbed sheet metal down the final stretch, Craven asked his crew, "Who won?" Answer: Craven, by two thousandths of a second, the closest finish in NASCAR history.

**PHOTOGRAPH BY NASCAR/AP**

# 3.23 FOOD CITY 500

BRISTOL MOTOR SPEEDWAY
**WINNER: KURT BUSCH**

A week after his narrow loss, Busch kept the drama to a minimum by leading the final 96 laps for his first win of the season. Afterward he rejoiced with this patriotic rubber-burning celebration.

**PHOTOGRAPH BY DON KELLY**

# 3.30 SAMSUNG/RADIO-SHACK 500

TEXAS MOTOR SPEEDWAY
**WINNER: RYAN NEWMAN**

Newman's decision to take just two new tires with 50 laps remaining turned out to be the correct call, even though Dale Earnhardt Jr. zipped past him on the restart. Newman reeled him in with 10 laps left.

**PHOTOGRAPH BY SUE OGROCKI/AP**

# 4.06 AARON'S 499

TALLADEGA SUPERSPEEDWAY
**WINNER: DALE EARNHARDT JR.**

Junior (8) grabbed a record fourth straight win at Talladega with a controversial late-race pass of Matt Kenseth. Upon review, NASCAR ruled that the pass occurred before the 8 car went below the yellow line.

**PHOTOGRAPH BY KARIM SHAMSI-BASHA**

**BEND IT LIKE . . .**
A CREWMAN FOR JEREMY MAYFIELD USED A LOW-TECH APPROACH TO FIX HIS BATTERED CAR AT TALLADEGA.

**PHOTOGRAPH BY KARIM SHAMSI-BASHA**

CATCH 24
WARD BURTON GOT CLOSE, BUT LIKE THE REST OF THE FIELD, HE NEVER WAS ABLE TO REEL IN JEFF GORDON (24) AT MARTINSVILLE.

PHOTOGRAPH BY SAM SHARPE

## 4.13 VIRGINIA 500

MARTINSVILLE SPEEDWAY
WINNER: JEFF GORDON

Gordon (DuPont Chevy) returned the favor to Bobby Labonte (18) from the Atlanta race in March, bumping him aside for the win. Said Labonte of the turnabout, "That was good, clean fun."

PHOTOGRAPH BY DON KELLY

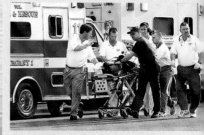

## 4.27 AUTO CLUB 500

CALIFORNIA SPEEDWAY
WINNER: KURT BUSCH

Busch's pit crew celebrates the first two-time winner of the year, made possible by his daring three-wide pass of Rusty Wallace with 12 laps to go. Asked Wallace, "Where the hell did he come from?"

PHOTOGRAPH BY WILL LESTER/AP

## 5.03 PONTIAC EXCITEMENT 400

RICHMOND INTERNATIONAL RACEWAY
WINNER: JOE NEMECHEK

The thoughts of the NASCAR world were with Jerry Nadeau, who crashed in a practice run and spent two weeks in a coma. He has made a slow recovery but is considering a return some time in '04.

PHOTOGRAPH BY RUSTY JARRETT/GETTY IMAGES

## 5.25 COCA-COLA 600

LOWE'S MOTOR SPEEDWAY
WINNER: JIMMIE JOHNSON

Johnson completed the fifth same-season double of Charlotte's marquee events, the Winston and the 600, but fans felt cheated by NASCAR's decision to end the race after 414 miles because of a brief downpour.

PHOTOGRAPH BY ALAN MARLER/AP

# 6.01 MBNA ARMED FORCES FAMILY 400

DOVER INTERNATIONAL SPEEDWAY
**WINNER: RYAN NEWMAN**

Newman's celebratory donuts were well earned: He muscled his 3,400-pound car around the Monster Mile without power steering for nearly half the race. Said the sore winner, "It pays good money to win."

**PHOTOGRAPH BY GEORGE TIEDEMANN/GT IMAGES**

# 6.08 POCONO 500

POCONO RACEWAY
**WINNER: TONY STEWART**

Unlike Ken Schrader (above), who crashed on Lap 8, Tony Stewart steered clear of trouble and snapped a careerlong 27-race winless skid after a string of strong but nonwinning runs.

**PHOTOGRAPH BY RUSS HAMILTON/AP**

# 6.15 SIRIUS 400

MICHIGAN INTERNATIONAL SPEEDWAY
**WINNER: KURT BUSCH**

After finishing last in both Michigan races as a rookie two years ago, Busch led the final 24 laps in his Rubbermaid Ford to give the automaker an early present the day before its 100th birthday.

**PHOTOGRAPH BY BRIAN CLEARY/ICON SMI**

# 6.22 DODGE/SAVE MART 350

INFINEON RACEWAY
**WINNER: ROBBY GORDON**

Gordon won the race but few friends when he broke a longstanding gentleman's agreement by passing teammate Kevin Harvick under the yellow. Harvick complained afterward that it was a "chicken move."

**PHOTOGRAPH BY ROBERT BECK**

## 7.05 PEPSI 400

DAYTONA INTERNATIONAL SPEEDWAY
**WINNER:** GREG BIFFLE

The caution flag brought on by this multicar smash involving Robby Gordon (left) and Mike Wallace on Lap 75 allowed Biffle to top off his gas tank, avoid an additional pit stop and cruise to victory.

**PHOTOGRAPH BY DARRYL GRAHAM/AP**

## 7.13 TROPICANA 400

CHICAGOLAND SPEEDWAY
**WINNER:** RYAN NEWMAN

Newman got the appropriate orange juice shower after taking the Tropicana. Kevin Harvick, meanwhile, ran out of gas with two laps to go in his bid for a third straight Chicagoland win.

**PHOTOGRAPH BY DONALD MIRALLE/GETTY IMAGES**

## 7.20 NEW ENGLAND 300

NEW HAMPSHIRE INTERNATIONAL SPEEDWAY
**WINNER:** JIMMIE JOHNSON

The repaved Loudon track helped drivers such as Dale Earnhardt Jr. (8) steer clear of trouble. Still, sixth-place finisher Junior couldn't catch Johnson, who stretched his final tank of gas for 93 laps.

**PHOTOGRAPH BY JON-PIERRE LASSEIGNE/AP**

## 7.27 PENNSYLVANIA 500

POCONO RACEWAY
**WINNER:** RYAN NEWMAN

Fans came to the Mountaintop seeking the autograph of the season's first four-time winner. Newman held off Kurt Busch, '03's only other three-time winner, by a scant .307 seconds.

**PHOTOGRAPH BY JAMIE SQUIRE/GETTY IMAGES**

**PIT BOSS** STRATEGIC STOPS AT DAYTONA HELPED MAKE ROOKIE GREG BIFFLE A WINNER FOR THE FIRST TIME ON THE WINSTON CUP CIRCUIT.

**PHOTOGRAPH BY RUSTY JARRETT/GETTY IMAGES**

# 8.03 BRICKYARD 400

INDIANAPOLIS MOTOR SPEEDWAY
**WINNER:** KEVIN HARVICK

Harvick, who had an autographed photo of four-time Indy 500 winner Rick Mears in the bedroom of his childhood home in Bakersfield, Calif., burns rubber on the way to Victory Lane after winning the 400.

**PHOTOGRAPH BY JOE ROBBINS**

# 8.10 SIRIUS AT THE GLEN

WATKINS GLEN INTERNATIONAL
**WINNER:** ROBBY GORDON

NASCAR has a new road-course sheriff, though his name is still Gordon. Robby joined Jeff as the only drivers to sweep Sonoma and Watkins Glen with a win that was—finally—free of controversy.

**PHOTOGRAPH BY MICHAEL ROMANO/ASP INC.**

# 8.17 GFS MARKETPLACE 400

MICHIGAN INTERNATIONAL SPEEDWAY
**WINNER:** RYAN NEWMAN

Newman (Alltel Dodge) won for the fifth time this year, but most of the excitement was generated after the race when Jimmy Spencer punched Kurt Busch, in a postrace scrap.

**PHOTOGRAPH BY SAM SHARPE**

# 8.23 SHARPIE 500

BRISTOL MOTOR SPEEDWAY
**WINNER:** KURT BUSCH

With Spencer parked for landing what many fans felt was a justified smack, Busch was greeted with jeers in Victory Lane—especially after spinning out Tennessee native Sterling Marlin along the way.

**PHOTOGRAPH BY JOE ROBBINS**

**DIG IT** DALE JARRETT OVERCAME THIS FORAY INTO A SAND TRAP TO DELIVER THE UPS FORD TO A SEVENTH-PLACE WATKINS GLEN FINISH.

**OLD FAITHFUL**
TIMEWORN BUT STILL FULL OF DOWN-HOME CHARM, DARLINGTON LOST ITS LABOR DAY SLOT TO THE NEW-AGE CALIFORNIA SPEEDWAY.

PHOTOGRAPH BY NIGEL KINRADE

## 8.31 MOUNTAIN DEW SOUTHERN 500

DARLINGTON RACEWAY
WINNER: TERRY LABONTE

On a nostalgic weekend—the last running of the Southern 500 during its traditional Labor Day slot—the 46-year-old, two-time Winston Cup champ celebrated his first win in 157 starts.

PHOTOGRAPH BY SAM SHARPE

## 9.06 CHEVY ROCK & ROLL 400

RICHMOND INTERNATIONAL RACEWAY
WINNER: RYAN NEWMAN

Another Newman win was overshadowed by postrace fireworks as an irate Kevin Harvick and his pit crew treated Ricky Rudd's car like a jungle gym after Rudd had punted him into the wall.

PHOTOGRAPH BY PHIL CAVALI/AP

## 9.14 SYLVANIA 300

NEW HAMPSHIRE INTERNATIONAL SPEEDWAY
WINNER: JIMMIE JOHNSON

Johnson prevailed despite a scary moment on pit lane when Jeff Gordon—co-owner of Johnson's car—bumped three members of the number 48 crew. Luckily they escaped serious injury.

PHOTOGRAPH BY DAVE ROLLS/ASP INC.

## 9.21 MBNA AMERICA 400

DOVER INTERNATIONAL SPEEDWAY
WINNER: RYAN NEWMAN

The winner pulled away from the most famous—or infamous—pit crew in NASCAR. Newman again rode uncanny fuel mileage to another victory and a season sweep at Dover.

PHOTOGRAPH BY F. PEIRCE WILLIAMS/ASP INC.

## 9.28 EA SPORTS 500

TALLADEGA SUPERSPEEDWAY
**WINNER:** MICHAEL WALTRIP

Pole sitter Elliott Sadler's spectacular crash with six laps left (he was not hurt) set up a thrilling final dash won by Waltrip. It was his fourth career victory, all at two restrictor-plate tracks.

**PHOTOGRAPH BY DAN LIGHTON/AP**

## 10.05 BANQUET 400

KANSAS SPEEDWAY
**WINNER:** RYAN NEWMAN

The number 12 car's sixth win in 13 races fueled the furor over his superior gas mileage, with grumblings in the garage that included the dreaded c word. Replied Newman, "We don't cheat."

**PHOTOGRAPH BY LARRY SMITH/AP**

## 10.11 UAW-GM QUALITY 500

LOWE'S MOTOR SPEEDWAY
**WINNER:** TONY STEWART

Stewart turns donuts in the distance after zipping past second-place Newman in the final laps on four fresh tires. "It's about time the fastest car won the race," said Stewart. "This fuel stuff is getting old."

**PHOTOGRAPH BY WALTER ARCE/ASP INC.**

## 10.19 SUBWAY 500

MARTINSVILLE SPEEDWAY
**WINNER:** JEFF GORDON

The 24 car left Busch and the rest of the field behind, leading 311 of 500 laps for a sweep of the 2003 races at this bump-and-grind short track. Said Gordon, "I wish we ran here every weekend."

**PHOTOGRAPH BY GEORGE TIEDEMANN/GT IMAGES**

## 10.27 BASS PRO SHOPS MBNA 500

ATLANTA MOTOR SPEEDWAY
**WINNER:** JEFF GORDON

Rain delayed Gordon's third victory of 2003 (and second straight) by a day, but nothing could slow Matt Kenseth's march to the title. With 240 points, Kenseth upped his lead with three races left.

**PHOTOGRAPH BY SAM SHARPE**

## 11.02 CHECKER AUTO PARTS 500 PRESENTED BY HAVOLINE

PHOENIX INTERNATIONAL RACEWAY
**WINNER:** DALE EARNHARDT JR.

Earnhardt Jr. (Bud Chevy) was excited by his victory—"The best win of my career"—but no more than the female fan who flashed press members in the media center during his press conference.

**PHOTOGRAPH BY SAM SHARPE**

## 11.09 POP SECRET MICROWAVE POPCORN 400

NORTH CAROLINA SPEEDWAY
**WINNER:** BILL ELLIOTT

Matt Kenseth locked up the Series title at the Rock, but Elliott's pit crew also had plenty to celebrate in his last stop. The 48-year-old Elliott won the race in what he says is his final full-time season.

**PHOTOGRAPH BY PHIL CAVALI**

## 11.16 FORD 400

HOMESTEAD-MIAMI SPEEDWAY
**WINNER:** BOBBY LABONTE

The 18 car has smooth sailing, but Labonte's victory was possible because Bill Elliott blew a tire while leading on the final lap of the series finale—and the last for Winston as title sponsor.

**PHOTOGRAPH BY GEORGE TIEDEMANN/GT IMAGES**

# 6

## FAST STARTS

JAMIE MCMURRAY (LEFT) WAS THE 2003 NASCAR ROOKIE OF THE YEAR EVEN THOUGH HIS BEST FINISH IN A RACE WAS THIRD (AT BOTH THE BRICKYARD 400 AND THE SHARPIE 500). MCMURRAY WAS THE FIRST DRIVER SINCE THE LATE KENNY IRWIN IN 1998 TO WIN THE TOP ROOKIE PRIZE WITHOUT WINNING AT LEAST ONCE. HERE ARE THE PAST SIX ROOKIE OF THE YEAR RECIPIENTS, HOW THEY EARNED THE HONOR AND HOW THEY FARED THE FOLLOWING SEASON.

| YEAR | ROOKIE OF THE YEAR | RANK | STARTS | WINS | TOP 5 | TOP 10 | FOLLOWING SEASON | RANK | STARTS | WINS | TOP 5 | TOP 10 |
|------|--------------------|------|--------|------|-------|--------|------------------|------|--------|------|-------|--------|
| 2003 | Jamie McMurray | 13th | 36 | 0 | 5 | 13 | | ? | ? | ? | ? | ? |
| 2002 | Ryan Newman | sixth | 36 | 1 | 14 | 22 | | sixth | 36 | 8 | 17 | 22 |
| 2001 | Kevin Harvick | ninth | 35 | 2 | 6 | 16 | | 21st | 35 | 1 | 5 | 8 |
| 2000 | Matt Kenseth | 14th | 34 | 1 | 4 | 11 | | 13th | 36 | 0 | 4 | 9 |
| 1999 | Tony Stewart | fourth | 34 | 3 | 12 | 21 | | sixth | 34 | 6 | 12 | 23 |
| 1998 | Kenny Irwin | 28th | 32 | 0 | 1 | 4 | | 19th | 34 | 0 | 2 | 6 |

## CHANGING of the GUARD

NASCAR'S YOUNG GUNS HAVE TAKEN OVER. DURING THE 2003 SEASON 17 OF 36 RACES WERE WON BY DRIVERS UNDER THE AGE OF 30. JUST 20 YEARS AGO, ONLY FIVE OF THE 30 WINNERS WERE UNDER 30. HERE'S A LOOK AT THE MEDIAN AGE OF WINSTON CUP RACE VICTORS ALONG WITH THE OLDEST AND YOUNGEST DRIVERS WHO WON ON THE CIRCUIT IN EACH OF THESE FIVE SEASONS.

BUSCH

SHEPHERD

| YEAR | MEDIAN AGE | OLDEST WINNER | YOUNGEST WINNER |
|------|-----------|---------------|-----------------|
| 2003 | 30 years, 4 days | Bill Elliott (48 years, 1 month, 1 day) | Kurt Busch (24 y, 7 m, 19 d) |
| 1998 | 31 y, 13 d | Dale Earnhardt (46 y, 9 m, 17 d) | Jeff Gordon (26 y, 6 m, 8 d) |
| 1993 | 36 y, 8 m, 8 d | Morgan Shepherd (51 y, 4 m, 27 d) | Davey Allison (32 y, 10 d) |
| 1988 | 32 y, 10 m, 27 d | Bobby Allison (50 y, 10 m, 11 d) | Davey Allison (27 y, 5 m, 27 d) |
| 1983 | 39 y, 10 m, 24 d | Richard Petty (45 y, 8 m, 11 d) | Terry Labonte (26 y, 11 m, 14 d) |

## IRON MAN

LAST SEASON RICKY RUDD STRETCHED HIS RECORD OF CONSECUTIVE STARTS TO 716. THREE DRIVERS ENTER THE 2004 SEASON WITH AT LEAST 500 CONSECUTIVE STARTS, INCLUDING RUSTY WALLACE, WHO COULD MOVE INTO SECOND PLACE ON THE ALLTIME LIST ON OCT. 16 AT LOWE'S MOTOR SPEEDWAY. HERE ARE THE ALLTIME LEADERS.

**1 RICKY RUDD**
716 STARTS
Jan. 11, 1981–active

**2 TERRY LABONTE**
655 STARTS
Jan. 14, 1979–Aug. 5, 2000

**3 DALE EARNHARDT**
648 STARTS
Sept. 9, 1979–Feb. 25, 2001

**4 RUSTY WALLACE**
625 STARTS
Feb. 19, 1984–active

**5 KEN SCHADER**
580 STARTS
Feb. 17, 1985–July 27, 2003

**6 RICHARD PETTY**
513 STARTS
Nov. 14, 1971–March 19, 1989

**7 MARK MARTIN**
509 STARTS
Feb. 14, 1988–active

RUDD

# NASCAR BY THE

## PONTIAC'S GREATEST MOMENTS IN NASCAR HISTORY

### 1950 February 5

Pontiac makes its first foray into NASCAR racing when Will Albright and Dick Clothier enter the 1950 Daytona Beach Race. Albright wins $50 for finishing 19th and completing 43 of the 48 laps, while Clothier finishes just five laps, ends up in 36th place and takes home $25.

### 1957 February 17

Shortly after the Pontiac Bonneville is unveiled during Speed Week in Daytona Beach, Cotton Owens drives one to victory on the Beach & Road Course for Pontiac's first NASCAR victory.

### 1962 February 18

Fireball Roberts wins the Daytona 500. Pontiacs dominated the circuit in '61 and '62, with drivers like Roberts and Jack Smith winning 52 of 105 races.

SMITH

## THEY BUILT EXCITEMENT

PONTIAC HAS BEEN INVOLVED WITH NASCAR RACING FOR MORE THAN 50 YEARS, BUT IN 2004, THE ONLY CARS BEARING THAT NAME ON THE NEXTEL CIRCUIT WILL BE IN PARKING LOTS. IN ALL, PONTIACS HAVE WON 154 TIMES, INCLUDING LAST MARCH AT DARLINGTON, WHEN RICKY CRAVEN CROSSED THE FINISH LINE INCHES AHEAD OF KURT BUSCH FOR PONTIAC'S FINAL TRIP TO VICTORY LANE. HERE ARE THE TOP CAR COMPANIES IN TERMS OF ALLTIME WINS AT NASCAR'S HIGHEST LEVEL.

**FORD** — 539 wins
LAST CHAMPION: MATT KENSETH (2003)

**CHEVROLET** — 513 wins
LAST CHAMPION: JEFF GORDON (2001)

**PLYMOUTH** — 190 wins
LAST CHAMPION: RICHARD PETTY (1972)

**DODGE** — 170 wins
LAST CHAMPION: RICHARD PETTY (1974)

**PONTIAC** — 154 wins
LAST CHAMPION: TONY STEWART (2002)

## IT'S NOT ABOUT THE MONEY

FOR THE FIRST TIME IN 18 YEARS THE WINSTON CUP CHAMP WAS NOT THE LEADING MONEY WINNER. MATT KENSETH'S WINNINGS PLACED HIM 13TH ON THE MONEY LIST—THE LOWEST-EVER FINISH FOR A POINTS CHAMP. HERE ARE THE OTHER WINNERS WHO WERE BEATEN OUT FOR THE MONEY TITLE.

ROBERTS

| YEAR | CHAMPION | WINNINGS (MONEY RANK) | MONEY LEADER | WINNINGS (CHAMPIONSHIP RANK) |
|---|---|---|---|---|
| 2003 | Matt Kenseth | $4,038,120 (13th) | Jimmie Johnson | $5,517,850 (2nd) |
| 1985 | Darrell Waltrip | $1,318,375 (2nd) | Bill Elliott | $2,383,186 (2nd) |
| 1973 | Benny Parsons | $182,321 (5th) | Cale Yarborough | $267,513 (2nd) |
| 1972 | Richard Petty | $339,405 (2nd) | Bobby Allison | $348,939 (2nd) |
| 1968 | David Pearson | $133,065 (2nd) | Cale Yarborough | $138,051 (17th) |
| 1966 | David Pearson | $78,194 (2nd) | Richard Petty | $94,666 (3rd) |
| 1963 | Joe Weatherly | $74,624 (2nd) | Fred Lorenzen | $122,587 (3rd) |
| 1961 | Ned Jarrett | $41,056 (5th) | Rex White | $56,395 (2nd) |
| 1958 | Lee Petty | $26,565 (2nd) | Fireball Roberts | $32,218 (11th) |
| 1954 | Lee Petty | $21,127 (2nd) | Herb Thomas | $29,974 (2nd) |
| 1950 | Bill Rexford | $6,175 (5th) | Johnny Mantz | $10,835 (6th) |

KENSETH
NASCAR Winston Cup Series

## NUMBERS

A sampling of racing facts and figures as the Winston Cup and Pontiac eras come to the finish line
**Compiled by David Sabino**

**1981 April 26**
A Pontiac driven by Morgan Shepherd finishes the Virginia 500 15 seconds ahead of Neil Bonnett's Ford, snapping an 18-year winless streak for the manufacturer.

**1983 February 20**
After crashing his Chevrolet during qualifying, Cale Yarborough wins the Daytona 500 in a number 28 Hardee's Pontiac.

**1984 July 4**
Driving the STP number 43 Pontiac Grand Prix, Richard Petty wins the Firecracker 400 at Daytona. It is his fifth career win in a Pontiac and the 200th and final victory of his career.

**1989 September 10**
Rusty Wallace wins the Miller High Life 400, the sixth victory of the season. The '89 points champion earned 20 top 10 finishes in 29 races.

**2002 November 16**
Tony Stewart becomes Pontiac's second Winston Cup champion in three years, following his teammate Bobby Labonte's win in 2000.

PETTY

STEWART

# SUPPORT

# ING CAST

Although a car has only one driver, it truly takes a village to be competitive in NASCAR. From team owners to video wizards to tire men, racing is a team sport

# FORTUNATE SOUL

## Rescued from a plane crash by a former Marine, Jack Roush cheated death and scaled racing's highest peak
### by Lars Anderson

THE UNMARKED police car weaves in and out of the heavy Richmond traffic, occasionally veering onto the highway shoulder and whipping up dust as it speeds toward the airport seven miles southeast of town. Riding shotgun is 60-year-old Jack Roush, sitting uncharacteristically quiet as he stares out the window from beneath one of his signature Panama hats. It's as if he's searching for something out there in the countryside, and in a way he is. These days Roush spends a lot of time pondering the meaning of life.

"I know the reason I'm living is to do something special, something good, with the time I have remaining," says Roush. "I'm just trying to figure out what that is."

As he sits here on this sunny September afternoon in 2002, Roush is in the midst of the finest run of success in his

decade and a half as a Winston Cup owner. One of his four drivers, Mark Martin, is gunning for the 2002 championship (he would finish a close second to Tony Stewart); two others, Kurt Busch and Matt Kenseth, are looking like solid bets to win future titles (in November 2003 Kenseth and Roush would celebrate their first championship as driver and owner); and the fourth, Jeff Burton, appears destined for another top 15 finish (he would finish 12th in 2002 and 12th in 2003). Despite the team's success, and the fact that the Chevrolet Monte Carlo 400 is starting in five hours, Roush is doing something blue-moon rare among Winston Cup owners: He's not giving racing one minute of thought. Roush, at his own request, is being steered through race-day traffic by a police officer so he will get to the airport in time to perform his most important task of the day. There he'll greet the man who, five months earlier, had saved his life.

JACK ROUSH was 16 the first time he cheated death. On a Saturday night in June 1958, dressed in his nicest pink shirt, Roush pulled his souped up '51 Ford out of his family's driveway in Manchester, Ohio, and headed north along winding Highway 136 toward the town of West Union, six miles away. There he was going to pick up a young lady and take her to a movie.

**PHOTOGRAPH BY CIA STOCK PHOTO**

**NEW LEASE ON LIFE**
ROUSH ADMITS TO BEING MORE PATIENT AFTER HIS BRUSH WITH DEATH, BUT HE SAYS HIS WILL TO WIN IS AS STRONG AS EVER.

About a third of the way to West Union, Roush, who was driving 50 mph, came up behind a car that was going 40. Roush immediately recognized the driver as Jim Bob Jenkins, who worked at the same automotive body shop at which Roush sanded and painted cars. Roush pulled opposite Jenkins, intending to pass him; Jenkins sped up. Roush slowed to let Jenkins go; Jenkins also slowed, not allowing Roush back in the lane. "That was it," says Roush. "The race was on."

**SUNNY-SIDE UP** ROUSH (BELOW, WITH HICKS) SUFFERED A COLLAPSED LUNG AND A BROKEN LEG WHEN THE EXPERIMENTAL AIRCAM CRASHED.

Soon the cars were going 80 mph through the summer dusk. Roush was nearly a car's length ahead when they reached a bend in the road. Seeing no oncoming headlights, Roush pressed forward. On the curve, though, Jenkins lost control of his car and bumped Roush

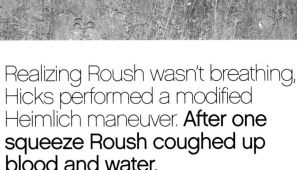

Realizing Roush wasn't breathing, Hicks performed a modified Heimlich maneuver. **After one squeeze Roush coughed up blood and water.**

onto the gravel shoulder, causing Roush to lose control of his car. "That's when it became panic time," says Roush.

Roush's Ford slid until it hit a dirt berm, which launched the car into the air. Spiraling like a football, it plunged into a ravine that had a shallow creek at its base. Roush, not wearing a seat belt, thought his Ford would land upside down, so he put his hands on the roof and wedged himself in tightly. Sure enough, the vehicle landed in the creek on its top then rolled a few times until it came to a stop on its wheels. Roush stepped out of the steaming car and into 12 inches of water without so much as a scratch on him.

Rather than deterring Roush from racing, the accident affirmed

his passion for it. "My parents grounded me for the next year, so I couldn't drive," says Roush. "That's when I realized how much I enjoyed cars and racing."

Fast forward to April 19, 2002. Roush Racing is now NASCAR's largest racing company, employing some 400 people and supporting four Winston Cup teams, two Busch Series teams and two Craftsman Truck Series teams. In two days four of those Winston Cup team would compete in the Aaron's 499 at Talladega, but on this day the teams' owner leaves the garage area at Talladega and boards his P-51 Mustang, a vintage World War II aircraft that he pilots 100 miles south to the airport in Troy. There, in a private hangar, some friends of Roush's have gathered to celebrate his 60th birthday. Before the party starts, Roush asks a friend if he can fly his Aircam, a lightweight, experimental aircraft. Minutes later Roush is in the air, savoring the peacefulness of the countryside on a cloudless evening.

Shortly after 6 p.m., as he passes over a small lake, Roush pulls back on the throttle to lift the plane. But above and behind the trees is a set of high-tension power lines. Roush doesn't have a chance. The plane barrels straight into the lowest line and the right wing is sheared off, causing the plane to nose-dive 75 feet straight into four feet of water.

Larry Hicks, 52, had finished his shift as a state game warden and was flipping on his television when, through his living room window, he saw the plane plunge into the water. A former sergeant major in the Marines who had been trained in the search and rescue of pilots downed in water, he immediately leaped into action. After telling his wife to call 911, Hicks jumped into his fishing boat and motored to the plane, which was half submerged and leaking fuel. He dived into the water and, within two minutes, had pulled an unconscious Roush out of the plane. Realizing Roush wasn't breathing, Hicks performed a modified Heimlich maneuver. After one squeeze Roush coughed up blood and water. Hicks then performed CPR until Roush began breathing. Paramedics rushed him to a nearby hospital, where Roush was discovered to have suffered a shattered left femur, a broken left ankle and a collapsed right lung. He was hospitalized for two weeks and then transported to a rehabilitation center near his home in Northville, Mich.

Six weeks after the accident Roush made his return to a NASCAR event, the May 31 MBNA Platinum 400 in Dover, Del. Never one to travel with an entourage, he parked his car in one of the outer lots and, by himself, hobbled on crutches toward the racetrack. As he began descending the stairs from the

**FLY GUY** ROUSH DIDN'T STOP DRIVING AFTER A NEAR-FATAL CAR WRECK, AND HE HASN'T GIVEN UP ON PILOTING HIS VINTAGE P-51 MUSTANG (RIGHT).

walkover bridge that leads into the infield, about 200 people recognized him. Fans, NASCAR officials, members of other teams all started cheering as if Caesar had entered the Colosseum.

Not surprisingly, Roush's near-death experience had a galvanizing effect on his teams. Not that they weren't determined before the accident—"The desire to win was always there," says Martin—but the accident suffused Roush Racing with a collective let's-do-it-for-Jack attitude. "We were all close before," says Kenseth, "but the accident forced us to become closer. We really wanted to run well for him."

In 2003 Kenseth didn't just run well for Roush, he was spectacular. Though Kenseth won only one race in '03, compared with his Winston Cup–high five W's in '02, he was easily the most consistent driver on the circuit, registering more top 10 finishes (25) than anyone else. Midway through the season Kenseth was asked a hypothetical question: If you win the championship, what's the first thing you'll do the moment you clinch? "That's easy," said Kenseth, "I'll take a long look at Jack. Everyone at Roush Racing knows how badly he wants a championship. He won't say that,

**A BIT OF BUBBLY**
KENSETH (WITH CHECK) LED ALL DRIVERS IN WINS DURING HIS THIRD YEAR WITH ROUSH AND WON THE SEASON POINTS TITLE IN HIS FOURTH.

bie Loomis, the crew chief for Jeff Gordon. "If he and his team can put it all together, and if Kurt doesn't let his emotions get out of control, I think it's just a matter of time before he wins a championship."

It's been Roush, of course, who has overseen the development of both Kenseth and Busch. As Roush recovered from his injuries in 2002, he was in frequent contact with his teams, offering advice and encouragement. This year he was back at the track full time, his presence an assuring one to his young drivers. "Having Jack back around is really uplifting," said Kenseth midway through the season. "He always seems to point us in the right direction."

"My will to win has never been stronger," Roush says. "Has this changed me? I'm the same person, except now I think I'm a little more patient."

ROUSH STANDS in the Richmond International Airport. He is waiting for the man he plans on seeing regularly the rest of his life. "Larry," Roush says softly as he hugs Hicks, "my guardian angel."

Sitting in the backseat of the unmarked police car, Roush and Hicks head to the track. That night, under the lights at Richmond, they watch Kenseth take the checkered flag. It's another glorious evening in the life of Jack Roush. □

## JACK'S GANG

**MATT KENSETH** 148 STARTS  7 WINS
*Mr. Consistency would like to repeat as Cup champion, as well as get a few more wins this season.*

**KURT BUSCH** 114 STARTS  8 WINS
*Though his trips to Victory Lane often drew boos from the crowd, a more mature Busch will certainly challenge for the points title.*

**JEFF BURTON** 332 STARTS  17 WINS
*The 36-year-old Burton is hoping to snap his 76-race winless streak in 2004.*

**MARK MARTIN** 566 STARTS  33 WINS
*Martin's eager to rebound from a sub-par 2003 season, in which he finished out of the top 10 for only the third time in 15 years.*

**GREG BIFFLE** 42 STARTS  1 WIN
*A points champ in both the Craftsman Truck and Busch series, Biffle hopes to build on his sizzling rookie campaign.*

but you can tell that's how he feels just by the look on his face whenever he talks about the possibility. It would be really special to give him his first championship."

While Busch was often overshadowed by Kenseth in 2003, he proved that his strong showing at the end of the '02 season was no fluke. He won four races this season, and though he earned the wrath of many fans for feuding with Jimmy Spencer, he's a popular pick in the garage to win the points championship in '04. "Kurt has all the talent in the world, and he's on a great team," says Rob-

**FORMIDABLE CREW** FEW TEAMS IN NASCAR CAN MATCH THE COMBINED TALENT OF (FROM LEFT) BUSCH, BIFFLE, KENSETH, BURTON, ROUSH AND MARTIN.

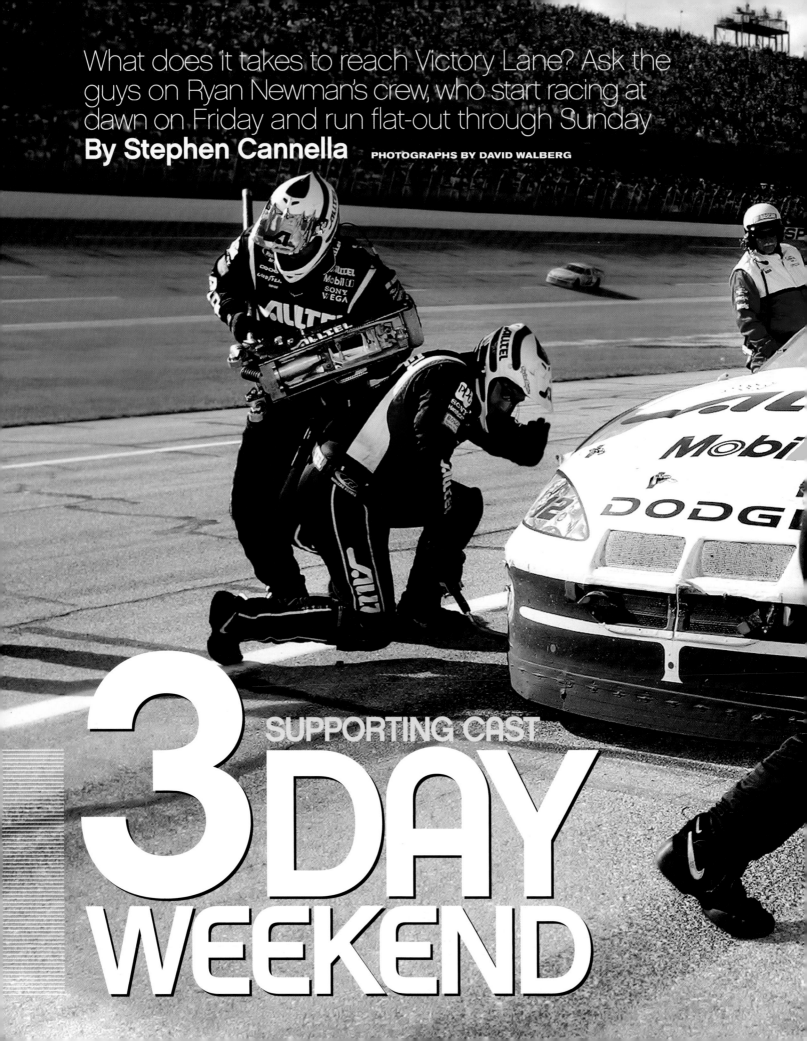

What does it takes to reach Victory Lane? Ask the guys on Ryan Newman's crew, who start racing at dawn on Friday and run flat-out through Sunday

**By Stephen Cannella**    PHOTOGRAPHS BY DAVID WALBERG

SUPPORTING CAST

# 3DAY WEEKEND

**STOP ACTION** IN 15 CHOREOGRAPHED SECONDS, NEWMAN'S CREW CAN GIVE THEIR MAN GAS AND FOUR NEW TIRES.

T O  T H E  naked eye Ryan Newman's third trip down pit road during the 2003 EA Sports 500 looked like a good one. It was a routine stop for fuel and new right-side tires, and his seven-man crew performed the frenzied ballet of the pits without any noticeable stumbles. A few whirs of the pneumatic wrench, several glug-glugs from two gasoline drums, and the number 12 car was back on the road a mere 10.72

seconds after it pulled into Pit Stall 2 at Talladega Superspeedway.

Of course, it's easier to follow a street hustler's hands than it is to catch the details of a pit stop in real time, which is why rear-tire carrier Trent Cherry went straight to the videotape at the conclusion of this one. All of Newman's race stops are recorded by a camera suspended above the pit stall. Several times during a race, Cherry, who doubles as the team's video coordinator, fires up the VCR in the war wagon—the high-tech toolshed and nerve center that stands just inside the pit wall—for up-to-the-minute efficiency reports.

Cherry's presence—not to mention that of a sophisticated video system—is an indication of how much the pit crew has evolved. A generation ago he would never have cracked the NASCAR gear-

Racing shop in Mooresville, N.C. Workouts are a daily staple when the team's not on the road; Cherry and trainer Bob Pressley designed a cross-training program heavy on upper-body work and flexibility.

With the exception of front-tire changer Dennis Terry, 31, who's a landscape architect during the week, the entire pit crew works full time in the shop. Jackman Chad Norris, 28, rear-tire changer Joe Piette, 37, and catch-can man Joe Moody, 32, double as mechanics. Front-tire carrier Ray Osian, 34, is in charge of tire maintenance. Cherry is, as he puts it, the "vehicular hygienist." He washes cars.

He also oversees the team's film study, an integral part of pit practice every afternoon. There's a mini pit row behind the shop complete with pit wall, three stalls and a fully stocked war wagon.

head culture. A former quarterback at Division II Lenoir-Rhyne College in Hickory, N.C., the 25-year-old freely admits he wouldn't know a camshaft from a carburetor. "A lot of these guys have been working on cars their whole lives," he says. "I don't claim to know anything about them."

He does know fraternity, film and fitness, though, all of which are as essential to life in the pits as earplugs. Most fans treat the Driver as a deity and give the men behind the men behind the wheel less attention than Shania Twain's bass player. But a driver can't have sustained success unless those faceless fire suits—the pit crew, the crew chief and the 10 or so behind-the-wall mechanics and attendants who go to every race—are a well-oiled machine. How many of Newman's circuit-leading eight victories in 2003 can his crew take credit for? "All of them," he says.

Team Newman's workweek begins every Tuesday at 7 a.m., when the crew gathers in the 1,000-square-foot weight room at the Penske

**IN THE HOUSE** AT TALLADEGA, A NASCAR INSPECTOR (RED SHIRT) CHECKED THE DIMENSIONS OF THE 12 CAR AS NEWMAN (CENTER) AND BORLAND (RIGHT) WATCHED. A MINOR INFRACTION LED TO SOME QUICK FENDER WORK (OPPOSITE).

Sessions begin with the racing equivalent of bunting practice: drills in such fundamentals as unscrewing lug nuts and rolling tires. "Most teams do fundamentals at the beginning of the year, and that's it," says Terry, who changed tires for several other drivers before Team Newman hired him six races into the 2003 season. "We do 30-minute fundamental drills every day before practice. It all becomes muscle memory."

It's also a chance to work on timesaving tricks like one Terry and tire-carrier Osian worked up for right-side-only stops. NASCAR rules say that the front-tire changer's air-powered wrench must be returned to the wall side of the car before the driver can leave the stall. Most front changers simply dash around the car when they've fastened their tire. But when he hits his last nut, Terry signals Osian, who has already carried the used rubber back to the wall, to jerk the air hose that connects from Terry's gun to the war wagon. The jackman drops the car when he sees Osian yank, the wrench flies

over the hood, and Newman zooms off before Terry even leaves his spot. "It saves us half a second to a second every time," Terry says. "We can be as fast on right-side changes as we can on the left."

For Sunday races Team Newman breaks camp on Thursday night, when most of the guys take the Penske jet to that weekend's site. (Because they have few mechanical responsibilities, Cherry, Terry and gas man Steve Berner fly in on Sunday morning.) SI spent a weekend with the number 12 team during last year's fall race at Talladega. The fans, all 150,000, saw Newman finish fourth after trailing by a lap for most of the race. This is what his crew saw.

### FRIDAY. QUALIFYING DAY.

**4:45 a.m.** The barbarians are at the gate—at least that's how the hordes of NASCAR officials who buzz around the racetrack every weekend must feel. Newman's road crew is huddled in a small fleet of rental cars outside the entrance to the Talladega infield. The crew members, along with the other 48 teams hoping to compete this weekend, are waiting for NASCAR to open the garage at 5:30. Says shocks specialist Pat Stufflet, "We're like a herd of cows."

Once inside, they'll unload the Intrepid from the Penske hauler, which was driven in from Mooresville the night before, set up their stall in the garage and prep the car for the NASCAR inspections that must be passed before qualifying this afternoon. In theory the predawn gate wait is a chance to talk strategy, but most of the team catches some z's. With a 14-hour day ahead, they'll need the rest.

**10:00.** There's a hang-up in the House, race-crew slang for the NASCAR inspection area. The Dodge's right quarter panel doesn't match NASCAR's template, so it's back to the garage. This problem is a bee sting compared to what the crew will deal with later, but for now it chaps 32-year-old crew chief Matt Borland no end. "It's the first time this year we haven't made it through right out of the box," he says.

**11:15.** The car has made it through the House, and Newman's ready for his first practice run. Mechanic Chris Allen, who's also in charge of driver comfort, straps Newman into the driver's seat, tightens his harness and makes sure the radio he'll use to communicate with Borland from the track is working. Tomorrow Allen will install the system he has rigged to keep Newman hydrated during the race: a hose that shoots Gatorade into the driver's mouth at the push of a button. "And it has to be green Gatorade," says Allen. "That's Ryan's go-juice."

> **SATURDAY** Checklist Set up gas can stand, gas weigher and gas probe box ✓ Replace 18v battery in reciprocating saw o

**2:15 p.m.** Things aren't right with the number 12 Dodge. During practice runs Newman noticed a slight engine vibration, and just 45 minutes before qualifying begins, the car is up on blocks with its wheels off. The crew is working feverishly to change the transmission—although Borland admits he's not sure that will solve the problem.

This is crunch time, because under NASCAR rules, if the engine

## "Changing engines is something you don't want to do," says Borland. "But better now than two laps into the race."

is altered once qualifying is over, Newman will have to start the race at the back of the pack. There's no time to take apart the motor, so everyone's fingers are crossed that a new transmission will make Newman's ride vibration free. Fortunately Newman is out of earshot when engine tuner John Payne says, "I just hope that nothing blows up."

**5:30.** The good news: Nothing blew up, and Newman qualified 12th. The bad news: The car's still not right. Borland doesn't want

to lose his starting position by tearing down the engine, so the crew is rushing to install a third transmission before NASCAR shuts down the garage. They have 90 minutes.

### SATURDAY. HAPPY HOUR.

**7:45 a.m.** Borland walks pit row to check out the stalls just as the sun begins to beat on the speedway. Teams are allowed to choose pit locations in the order they start the race, and a good stall can make or break a race. When Newman crashed during qualifying at Dover in 2002 and took a provisional, Borland skipped his Saturday stroll and picked a pit stall off the track map. Bad move. Several crew members tripped over a drainage ditch adjacent to the pit wall during the race, leading to a handful of bad stops.

Today Borland chooses Stall 2, near the exit end of pit row. It's a good one—not a drain in sight—with a short shot back onto the track. When Newman exits the pit on Sunday, he'll be able to gun it without having to fight through traffic on pit road.

**11:30.** Saturday-morning practice runs aren't just Sunday drives. Borland and chief engineer Mike Nelson use Newman's runs to calculate fuel mileage, which helps them map out when they'll pit during the race. They aren't thrilled with the mileage readings today, so Norris, Payne and company have installed a new carburetor.

The car was running hot, a problem that got a low-tech fix: Borland simply removed some of the duct tape covering the front grill so more air could flow over the engine. Newman, who has an engineering degree from Purdue, is usually ultraprecise in the feedback he gives the crew. (He reported that the water temperature was "229 degrees.") So the last comment that crackles over the radio when he pulls into the garage after his final practice run is ominously vague. "The engine felt a little funny," he says. "I'd like to get out there for one more feel before practice is over."

**2:00.** Newman wasn't imagining things: During a postpractice engine check Payne finds a burned-out piston. This is no dented fender. The motor must be removed and completely rebuilt.

It's bad enough that Newman will lose his starting spot, but there's a time crunch too. NASCAR will close his garage at four today, so Team Newman has 120 minutes to rebuild a car.

Before the piston was found, the crew was working to complete the checklists taped to every section of the car, itemizing what needed to be done. The checklists are abandoned now, and everyone helps with the engine. Even Newman, in jeans and a polo shirt, gets his hands dirty.

**4:00.** Borland is sweeping the floor of Garage 38 when a NASCAR official ambles by to close things down. Race prep is behind schedule, and Newman will start last, but the job is done. "Changing engines is something you definitely don't want to do," says Borland. "But you'd rather have it happen now than two laps into the race."

### SUNDAY. RACE DAY.

**7:00 am.** The Sunday guys have arrived. While some of the crew finishes the race-prep checklists in the garage, the jet-weary Cherry and Terry are part of a group that sets up the pit stall. The war wagon is wheeled out. It's equal parts entertainment center, tool cart and pantry: It's stocked with three computers; a satellite system; two flat-panel monitors; the dizzying array of gadgets needed to keep a race car running for 500 miles; and, on this day, a clutch of snacks that includes a pan of homemade Rice Krispies treats. Says Cherry, "You could live out of this thing."

**10:30.** The stall is set, and the crew kills time by signing autographs for fans strolling pit road before the race. Terry is on his haunches, gluing lug nuts on the 16 tires that have been laid out behind the wall like a giant checker set. Berner readies his gas cans and the scale he uses to weigh them after every stop. Those readings will tell the crew how much fuel the car is using.

**Noon.** An hour before the race and the crew is gathered in the hauler for a final strategy meeting. When it ends, everyone changes into fire suits and walks to the pit stall. Once there Terry and Piette, the tire changers, warm up by drilling lug nuts onto a wheel frame on the side of the war wagon. Others go through a stretching regimen, and when Borland arrives in the pit he fires up the troops with chest bumps and high fives. He, Nelson and Penske president Don Miller will follow the race and communicate with Newman from a command center atop the wagon. Shortly before the green flag waves, Miller's voice crackles over

**D-DAY** NEWMAN'S CREW MEMBERS MET WITH THEIR DRIVER (ABOVE, FAR LEFT) IN THE HAULER BEFORE THE RACE AND LATER, WITH SHREWD STRATEGY AND QUICK WORK (BELOW), HELPED HIM PLACE FOURTH THEN PACKED UP TO GO DO IT ALL AGAIN THE NEXT WEEK.

> **SUNDAY** Checklist | Install practice wheel ✓ Set up camera pole and camera ✓ Lay out wedge/trackbar wrenches ✓ Take prima

the race radio, "Good luck, Ryan, and drive it like you stole it."

The stall is quiet during the early laps. The crew follows the race on the war wagon TV and on a computer chart that lists every driver's lap speed and position. Newman's fiancée, Krissie Boyle, sits in a director's chair and scans other drivers' radios, listening in for strategy and word on track conditions. His father, Greg, who carries gas cans for Berner, sits on the wall and gazes across the track.

**Lap 10.** The reverie is broken when Larry Foyt crashes and the first yellow of the day flies. Caution laps are prime pitting opportunities, and Newman's crew scrambles.

Four laps later Newman cruises down pit road for four tires and gas, his first stop of the day. It takes 14.41 seconds, about average for this crew. Berner, who was promoted to gas man halfway through this season, is nearly shaking with excitement. "That was my first superspeedway stop," he says.

**Lap 16.** There isn't much time to regroup. With the caution still out Borland asks Newman to come back for more gas. He's barely used any since the last stop, but adding a gallon or two could shave a valuable second off a later stop.

**Lap 89.** Two laps after pitting for a fill-up and left-side tires, New-

## Newman is asked, How many of his eight race victories in 2003 can his crew take credit for? "All of them," he says.

man is back with more serious problems. A run-in with Kurt Busch bent his fender into the right front tire. Terry changes the tire while Osian hammers the fender back into place. By the time he gets back on the track Newman has lost a lap and slid to 31st place.

**Lap 125.** The mood in Stall 2 is grim. With 63 laps to go Newman is trying to fight his way to the front of the lap-down pack. A new NASCAR rule allows the leader of that group to get his lap back if there's a caution. Newman pits for the seventh time, and as he comes down pit road Borland tells him over the radio that he has to beat Michael Waltrip off pit road to preserve his position. The crew rushes through a four-tire and fuel stop. Berner and his gas can are nearly dragged along when Newman tears out just ahead of Waltrip.

**Lap 170.** The crew has taken to rooting on Penske teammate Rusty Wallace, who's challenging for the lead, when Newman gets his break. He has just taken the lead of the lap-down pack when Jeff Burton spins out and the caution waves. Stall 2 erupts. Newman pits for four new tires and fuel. When the racing resumes, with 14 laps to go, Newman is 24th and back in the race.

The final 14 laps are a blur, but for the most part his crew can sit back and admire his driving. Newman has worked his way near the front of the field when Elliott Sadler crashes and a red flag flies on Lap 182. Newman is in fifth place when the race restarts with four laps to go, and in a sprint to the finish he moves up one spot. "That's a biggie," he whoops to his ecstatic crew over the radio. "That's our first top five finish in a restrictor plate race."

The key word is *our*. □

# THE FIRST

Dale Sr. reigned supreme in NASCAR until a crash took his life in 2001. Today Dale Jr. is the sport's most magnetic star. The story of the Earnhardts is the story of racing in America

PHOTOGRAPH BY GEORGE TIEDEMANN/GT IMAGES

# FAMILY

REPRINTED FROM SPORTS ILLUSTRATED, FEBRUARY 6, 1995

## THE FIRST FAMILY

# THE BUSINESS OF BEING DALE

Alone at the apex of the sport he loved, Dale Earnhardt Sr. created an empire unrivaled in NASCAR
**by Ed Hinton**

DALE EARNHARDT sits on a sofa in his office, softly singing a line from a country-rock song: "I'm in a hurry, and I don't know why." At a nearby airport a Learjet awaits his daily dash to somewhere, while across from Earnhardt in the fax-and-FedEx-cluttered office, his agent is making what sounds like a deal a minute on the horn, and in an outer office secretaries are answering the phone with, "Good afternoon. Dale Earnhardt Incorporated."

The 43-year-old man on the sofa bears only a vague resemblance to the ninth-grade dropout from the textile mill town of Kannapolis, N.C., who in his youth would wreck other dirt-trackers for grocery money. But the words he is singing hit home, for Earnhardt has always seemed to be in a hurry without knowing why. Now, though, his status has at last caught up with his manner.

He is surrounded by stacks of picture postcards and cases of trading cards—today's shipment to fulfill mailed-in requests. No, yesterday's. "I'm this many behind," he says. His right hand is a blur, autographing at perhaps three times the rate of Richard Petty, the gentler man whom Earnhardt has replaced as the supreme figure of the NASCAR faithful.

He sings some more: "I don't know where I'm goin'."

Sitting there on the desk of the agent with the perfect name, Don Hawk, are 308 new requests for personal appearances, and only the ones for 1996 and beyond have a prayer. Filed in the outer office are thousands of charity requests—fulfilled, yet to be fulfilled, unfulfillable, even bizarre. Take the widow "who wanted me to drive the hearse for her husband's funeral," Earnhardt says. Did he do it? A prolonged expletive serves as a no.

Such has been the deluge upon these offices since October 1994, when Earnhardt clinched his seventh NASCAR season championship, tying Petty's lifetime record. Not long ago that mark was widely considered unapproachable. Now Earnhardt is

**HARD DRIVER**
EARNHARDT'S IMAGE WAS FORMED IN THE '70S, WHEN HE WOULD FREQUENTLY WRECK HIS COMPETITORS FOR GROCERY MONEY.

**PHOTOGRAPH BY DOZIER MOBLEY**

**RACING LEGACY**

AFTER HIS FATHER, RALPH, DIED OF A HEART ATTACK IN 1973, A 22-YEAR-OLD DALE WAS LEFT TO LEARN TO RACE ON HIS OWN.

team, Richard Childress Racing, whose primary sponsor is GM Goodwrench.

Hawk hawks his hot commodity as "the Michael Jordan of his sport," and endorsement seekers want Earnhardt's name on everything from hunting knives to private jets. "We've got what we think is the hottest property in motor sports in the world," Hawk says. Agent hype or not, Hawk may be right, considering the death in May 1994 of Formula One's worldwide idol, Ayrton Senna.

In December 1994 *Forbes* magazine estimated Earnhardt's personal income at $5.5 million a year, but—considering his salary, bonuses, 50% share of winnings and an average 25% of wholesale souvenir sales—the figure might be more reasonably estimated at $14 million. And if you throw in endorsements, revenues from poultry farming and cattle ranching, and income from a Chevrolet dealership, Earnhardt's annual take could be as high as $20 million.

For fans the price of living vicariously through Earnhardt varies. You can buy a piece of his intimidating life for anywhere from $1 (a bumper sticker) to $5,500 (a custom leather jacket). In between, says Hawk, are "the different T-shirts, earrings, belts, belt buckles, suspenders, socks, sweatshirts, jackets, hats, plaques, pictures, postcards, toy cars, clocks, watches, key chains. Man, we've got it all covered. And the fans want a little bit of everything."

The $5,500 jacket is only temporarily the high-end item, Hawk

expected—even by Petty, who retired in 1992—to break and then obliterate the record with an eighth, a ninth, maybe a 10th championship. NASCAR has a new kind of king.

Earnhardt's bad-boy mystique has thrown a shadow as dark as his racing colors over the old folk heroism of the patient, easygoing King Richard. Gone from the teeming infields of the racetracks are the red-and-blue flags bearing the sport's formerly most popular number, Petty's 43. Now there are seas of black flags emblazoned with Earnhardt's fiercely forward-thrust 3.

Earnhardt built his reputation as a predator during the mid- and late '80s, when he left other drivers wrecked and outraged in his wake. And though he has since mellowed on the track, he still rides the image: The Intimidator, he is widely called, or the Man in Black.

The public is buying the image. Earnhardt is raking in the bucks at a rate Petty never imagined. The $1.77 million

**TRIPLE THREAT**

EARNHARDT WON THE FIRST OF HIS SEVEN POINTS TITLES IN ROD OSTERLUND'S NUMBER 2 CHEVY, BUT HE WILL BE FOREVER IDENTIFIED WITH THE NUMBER 3 CAR HE DROVE FOR RICHARD CHILDRESS (HERE DUELING WITH PETTY, NEAR RIGHT).

in bonuses Earnhardt received for winning the 1994 Winston Cup is almost paltry next to the income of his grassroots empire, Dale Earnhardt Inc., and its partner companies, which in '93 grossed an estimated $42 million in souvenir sales alone. Earnhardt's numbers for '94 aren't all in, and anyway he and Hawk—a nondenominational minister who, as vice president and general manager of DEI, negotiates Earnhardt's contracts—aren't telling. But it's reasonable to guess that in the driver's record-tying season, his souvenir sales surpassed $50 million.

More than 10,000 General Motors dealerships nationwide sell Earnhardt items. Over the course of a year various all-Earnhardt catalogs list 749 items. In a 1995 QVC appearance Earnhardt sold $900,000 worth of merchandise in less than two hours. That almost matched his base salary of a bit more than $1 million from his

adds. Soon, certified race-worn Earnhardt helmets and driving uniforms will go on sale, and there's so little feel for what the market will bear that Earnhardt's contract with Scorecard, a major marketer of memorabilia, does not yet specify their price. The only gauge for projection is that Earnhardt uniforms have been sold at charity auctions for as much as $10,000.

Identification with Earnhardt may be based on something as simple as the anger on the nation's expressways. This is the opinion of Charlotte Motor Speedway president H.A. (Humpy) Wheeler, the savviest promoter in stock car racing, who built his success on his ability to read the psyches of NASCAR fans, both hard-core and fringe. "I think everybody in the country is angry about having to drive in urban areas," says Wheeler. "They hate the traffic with a passion. Earnhardt drives through traffic too. And he won't put up

with anything. He's going to get through. And that's what they want to do—but they can't. So Earnhardt is playing out their fantasies."

Then there's the general surliness of our society, a public with an attitude that mirrors Earnhardt's attitude. Whereas Petty was always out among his fans, mingling, signing autographs, talking amiably with anyone who approached him, Earnhardt rarely shows his face at a track for longer than it takes to walk hurriedly from his private motor coach to his race car. He displays a testy reluctance to do interviews or make unpaid promotional appearances. Even that, Wheeler believes, has made him popular, particularly in the South.

"Earnhardt is the resurrected Confederate soldier," says Wheeler. "Where Petty was always compliant, Earnhardt will stand his ground and say, 'I'm not going to do that.' And the people who love him are the people who are told, every day, what to do and what not to do, and they've got all those rules and regulations to go by. That just draws them closer to him."

*Close* might not be the right word. When Atlanta Motor Speedway general manager Ed Clark threw a relatively small cocktail party for Earnhardt in 1993, "Earnhardt sat on one side of the room and the fans sat on the other, and they just sort of looked at each other," Clark recalls. "Even the ones bold enough to go over and get their pictures taken with Earnhardt would pose with him quickly and then move on—as if they were all afraid he was going to punch them or something."

During his own reign, Petty says, "everybody felt at ease with me—the President of the United States, the drunkest cat at the racetrack and everybody in between. With Earnhardt, there's a love-hate relationship." But, Petty adds, "destiny is a funny thing. The right people come along at the right times."

**EMPIRE MAKER**

THE DEMANDS OF HIS CAREER MADE IT HARD FOR EARNHARDT TO BALANCE FUN (LIKE HUNTING, TOP) AND FAMILY (FROM LEFT: DAUGHTER KELLY, DALE JR. AND WIFE TERESA) WITH OFF-TRACK OBLIGATIONS FOR HIS FANS.

Earnhardt has been a hard man, a man of and for harsh times, since the ninth grade—when, as he once put it, he "couldn't hang, man, couldn't hang." He was always in a hurry, never knowing why. "Never dreamed much," he says.

He came up far harder than Petty, who stepped into a well-established racing team with his famous father, Lee. Earnhardt, too, was from a racing family, but his father, Ralph, a maestro of the Carolina short tracks, died of a heart attack in 1973, leaving Dale to race on his own at age 22.

By 1975, when Petty was in his prime, Earnhardt and his young family "probably should have been on welfare," he once said. "We didn't have money to buy groceries." By the age of 24 he was with his second wife and had three children. He'd married first at 17, had a son, Kerry, then divorced, then allowed his ex-wife and her new husband to adopt Kerry because, he said, "I couldn't afford to make the child-support payments."

Then, he continued, "racing cost me my second marriage because of the things I took away from my family." He and his second wife, Brenda, had a daughter, Kelly, and a son, Dale Jr., but the race car always came first. "For our family cars, we drove old junk Chevelles—anything you could get for $200," Earnhardt said. He would borrow a few hundred dollars on Thursday to buy racing tires and parts, gambling that he would win enough money on Friday and Saturday nights to repay the loan on Monday.

Wrecking other drivers wasn't gratuitous mischief—it was what Earnhardt felt he had to do to get by. And the instinct stuck with him. During his first nine years in the Winston Cup Series, beginning in 1979, when he was Rookie of the Year, his reputation for wildness on the track grew. "With Earnhardt," said archrival Darrell Waltrip, "every lap is a controlled crash."

In 1987 Earnhardt won 11 races and his third Winston Cup, but he wrecked so many other drivers along the way, inclining so many of his furious peers to payback, that even the mild-mannered Petty predicted, "There'll come a Sunday when there won't be enough wreckers to pick up the pieces of his car."

victories and will almost certainly never approach Petty in that department. During Petty's first 14 seasons, 1958 through '71, the NASCAR schedule included 40, 50, even 60 races a year. The '95 Winston Cup schedule has only 31. So Earnhardt will never have the statistical opportunities Petty had. "He might have won 300 races," Petty says, "if he'd come along when I did."

Petty usually made a spectacle of a NASCAR race only at the end: He ran conservatively, waited for attrition, then made his move in the final few miles. Earnhardt makes it a show all the way. Whether he actually wins a race is almost irrelevant to the spectators, whose pulses he makes pound all afternoon. Earnhardt turns a black Chevrolet into 3,500 pounds of virtual athlete, catching the draft with seat-of-the-pants instinct, with pure feel for the turbulent air around him and the cars brushing his. He finds grooves where traction seems nonexistent, and he regularly gets in and out of jams no other driver could escape.

Some say Earnhardt is the best there has ever been in NASCAR. But, says Petty, "there's never the best. There's always a faster gun." What is clear is that Earnhardt is head and shoulders above the rest of the current drivers.

"I had a better supporting cast," says Petty. "I had [David] Pearson." The retired Pearson remains second to Petty on the alltime wins list, with 105. "About half a tick behind Pearson were [Cale] Yarborough [83 career wins] and [Bobby] Allison [84 wins]." Earnhardt's lack of stellar competition "is not his fault," adds Petty. "It's just the circumstances."

So here sits Earnhardt, alone at the pinnacle of his sport, rolling

## Whether he actually wins a race is almost irrelevant to the spectators, **whose pulses he makes pound all afternoon.**

Earnhardt shrugged and smirked and accused all the other drivers of crying. "They ain't ever seen the kind of rough racing I've had to do in my life just to survive," he said. "They don't want to mess with this ol' boy." There it was: the direct tug on the heartstrings of an angry, hard-knocks segment of workaday America. Earnhardt's words could have come straight from a Hank Williams Jr. song.

The War of 1987—Earnhardt versus all the rest—ended after he was called on the carpet by NASCAR president Bill France Jr., who gave him a private warning that must have gotten through: Since then Earnhardt has steadily cleaned up his driving act. But the bad-boy image abides and looms, because every fan and every NASCAR driver knows that Earnhardt can still win a fender scuffle should the need arise.

He is "a pure driver," says Petty, who quickly adds, "I never claimed to be a great driver. All I wanted to be known as was a winner." Petty won by calculation, finesse and superior financing. He turned out victories like manufactured products—200 during his career, still a NASCAR record. Earnhardt has only 63 Winston Cup

in money and still hungry after all these years. Still in a hurry without knowing why.

How much money is enough?

"Ain't counting money," he grouses. "Ain't counting it by the dollar. I'm counting it by what's the next race. I want to win the next race. The next race is the Daytona 500. I've never won it. I've won 24 races at the Daytona Speedway. More races there than anybody else, ever. But I've never won the Daytona 500."

The greatest oddity in NASCAR racing is that its best driver has never won its biggest race. But just after indicating that this sticks in his craw, Earnhardt snaps, "It bothers y'all [the media]. It don't bother me. I'm still confident that I've got several shots to win it."

In recent years Earnhardt has been the dominant force of Daytona Speed Week each February, running away with various preliminary races and then dominating the 500 itself—until the final laps. In 1990, his nearest miss, he commanded the race for almost exactly 499 miles and then ran over debris that cut one of his tires and allowed then unknown Derrike Cope to slip past him and win.

(And even at that moment of dumbfounding defeat, Earnhardt was spectacular, saving his fishtailing car from what appeared to the passing Cope to be a certain crash.)

Since then every Daytona 500 has been the same song, different verse. Last year Earnhardt's late-breaking problem was that his car just didn't handle well. Being so consistently strong at Daytona, controlling everything that can be controlled, "you gotta win it sometime," Earnhardt says. And so, at least in his quest to win the biggest stock car race there is, he has a reason to remain in a hurry.

Back in his office, in a corner of his 400-acre farm near Mooresville, N.C., Earnhardt wonders aloud if there'll be time to pack a bag for wherever the Lear is about to take him today. (His leather-bound datebook says it's Atlanta.) He continues to turn out the lightning autographs, concentrating now on the trading cards, and suddenly he sends one flying out of the stack and onto the coffee table, saying, "Hey, Don!"

Hawk examines it. "That's a bootleg card," he says.

Earnhardt has contracts with six trading-card companies, and he autographs cards by the "thousands and thousands and thousands," he says. But this lean, mean signing machine has a laser eye for one little unlicensed card in a box with hundreds of licensed ones.

"If you endorse it, you're saying it's legal," says Hawk. "Somebody got Dale to sign one of these [he holds up a picture postcard] at a racetrack, put it on a laser machine, and now they've turned it into

worn-out felt-tip pen and says, "I'm out of time, but I'll keep talking." He stretches out on the sofa, resigning himself to a few more minutes of interview.

To have known him since 1979 is to sense right now that "Earnhardt is antsy," as the late Joe Whitlock often put it. Whitlock was Earnhardt's original image maker, aide-de-camp, adviser, handler, nurturer, even coddler. The brattish young driver was restless, idiosyncratic, unpolished, bewildered by his sudden transition from small time to big time. Whitlock babied him, became almost his surrogate father, and he created an image for Earnhardt in the media—even landed him on the front page of *The New York Times* sports section in 1980, when that realm was virtually unreachable for NASCAR.

"Earnhardt's antsy—let's go,"

## Earnhardt's bad-boy mystique **has thrown a shadow as dark as his racing colors** over the old folk heroism of the patient, easygoing King Richard.

a trading card. There's no contract, no agreement with anybody."

"Fans send that stuff in to get it signed, and I can't sign it, and they get mad," says Earnhardt.

In rushes a courier from Sports Image Inc., the major distributor of Earnhardt souvenirs, with a bootleg poster the company's scouts have caught. "You can sue those people," Earnhardt tells the man. "You gotta get those guys. Sports Image sells our posters. It's Sports Image's damn responsibility to pursue that sumbitch. If I'm gonna have to pursue it, I'm gonna start doing those posters myself!" (This is no idle threat. In the coming weeks Earnhardt would buy out Sports Image and make himself CEO.)

"They just wanted you to see it," says the courier.

"Seeing ain't gonna fix it," Earnhardt snaps. "Ask Hawk. I don't want to talk about it."

Jeez. Pulling in as much money as Earnhardt and Hawk do, why are they so upset about one little counterfeit trading card and one bootleg poster?

"The black market in NASCAR," says Hawk, "has got to be worth several million dollars a quarter—in pictures, plaques, die-cast cars, collectibles."

Still—stacked up against $42 million?

"They must be countin' up all that bootleg ----," Earnhardt says. Done at last with the day's autographing, Earnhardt drops a

Whitlock would command the driver's entourage when he sensed that Earnhardt was in a hurry without knowing why. So it went for a decade, until Whitlock, a hard-drinking, old school NASCAR star maker, could no longer keep pace with the Earnhardt phenomenon and its new corporate handlers.

To have known Earnhardt and his circle since 1979, to have seen the way it was then and the way it is now, is to feel compelled to ask, "Do you ever think of Whitlock?"

Earnhardt closes his eyes. "All the time," he says.

The more Whitlock felt passed by—by what even Earnhardt says "sometimes feels like a runaway train"—the more he drank. The more he drank, the more the corporate sponsors cut him off from Earnhardt. Just before Christmas 1989, Whitlock was shuffled off the Earnhardt-Goodwrench team, leaving him without a solid source of income.

"Joe held to his belief that once Dale knew of this, he would straighten it out—let them all know that Joe would indeed be involved, as he had been from the beginning," says Whitlock's widow, Hud. But "there wasn't much contact" with Earnhardt after Whitlock was shut out, she says. "So many others were involved, and communications were channeled through so many directions. Joe took it so personal. The business loss bothered him, because we were in financial trouble, but not as much as the loss of Dale himself."

was battling for the lead, Whitlock walked out to his side yard with a 12-gauge shotgun, knelt down and blew off the back of his head.

Earnhardt lies on the sofa with his eyes closed. He says, "Ralph Earnhardt, Joe Whitlock, Neil Bonnett [Dale's closest friend among drivers, killed in a crash at Daytona on Feb. 11, 1994]. That's the toughest part of my mental life. You lose your dad, whom you idolized, who taught you everything you know. Then you lose a close friend who you weren't close enough to, who helped you so much in your life. Then you lose a close friend who shared so much with you. It's really been tough. Those are the three toughies in the life of Dale Earnhardt."

He gets up and walks to an outer office and has a secretary pull open the file drawers full of charity requests. "I don't have time for family life," he says somberly of his third wife, Teresa, and their six-year-old daughter, Taylor. He returns to the sofa and sits, though he gives a sense that it's almost time to go.

It seems a million years, he is told, since that afternoon at Atlanta in 1978, when an unknown kid got a one-shot ride with Osterlund Racing and during the race was slammed by veteran Dave Marcis, whereupon he slammed Marcis back without so much as a serious swerve, attracting the attention of Joe Whitlock.

"Damn! Look at Earnhardt's kid!" Whitlock boomed up in the press box, identifying Dale in the only way anyone else would recognize: as the son of the old dirt-tracker Ralph Earnhardt. Whitlock took Earnhardt's kid under his wing and made him Earnhardt, "taught me that there's more to racing than driving a car," as Dale said, and got him organized for the stardom that Whitlock swore would come. DEI was created in 1979. And the rest is. . . .

But there's no time to dwell on that. Gotta go. Still in a hurry. At least the Lear and the leather datebook give him reasons why. "I'm going home," he says, but just long enough "to pack my clothes."

He travels light, the only extra baggage being those "three toughies," the ghosts in the life of Dale Earnhardt.   □

"We were still friends," says Earnhardt. "Just not close enough friends. Not as close as we had been, in our time."

One of their final contacts, Hud recalls, was late in 1990, when Earnhardt phoned and asked Whitlock to meet him. But Whitlock came home from the meeting unexpectedly early, she says. "He said, 'Well, we said a few things.' But he said Dale seemed to be in a real hurry."

On May 6, 1991, left behind at age 55, Whitlock sat alone in his Lake Norman, N.C., house, on which he had received a foreclosure notice. The rest of the NASCAR traveling circus was at Talladega, Ala. Sometime during the live telecast of a race in which Earnhardt

# EPILOGUE

THREE YEARS *after this story ran in SI, Earnhardt experienced the most gratifying moment of his racing career. On Feb. 15, 1998, Earnhardt finally won the Daytona 500 after 19 tries. When he climbed out of his car in Victory Lane, the 46-year-old Earnhardt couldn't stop tears from leaking out of his cobalt eyes. "I've got that goddam monkey off my back!" he screamed.*

*Though he would remain tied with Richard Petty (with Earnhardt, in photo at left) with seven points championships, Earnhardt continued to race with a style and swagger befitting his intimidating image. He finished second in the Winston Cup standings in 2000 and had more top five finishes (13) than he'd had in the previous two seasons combined. He won 76 races over the course of his 27-year career in NASCAR and earned more than $41 million on the track.*

*Sadly, Earnhardt's life was cut short on Feb. 18, 2001. Seconds before the end of the Daytona 500, Earnhardt's Chevrolet Monte Carlo hit the wall entering Turn 4, and he was killed instantly. In an eyeblink NASCAR lost not only one of its best drivers but also the heart and soul of the sport.*

GEORGE TIEDEMANN/GT IMAGES (2)

117

# JUNIOR ACHIEVEMENT

After losing its top star, NASCAR found solace, and much more, in the emergence of Dale Earnhardt Jr.
**by Jeff MacGregor**

THE LINE snakes around the building, folding back again and again on itself. A labyrinth traced by sagging lengths of yellow poly police tape winds through the spears of palmetto and twists across the white-hot decorative gravel, then threads back between some leafless, blasted saplings before wandering all the way out past the molten parking lot until it turns again, back up the alley, hundreds of feet, into the last little rectangle of lifesaving shade left in Daytona Beach, where it loops the Dumpster twice and finally meanders, unmercifully, back out into that terrifying supertropical sunshine and along the malarial drainage ditch that parallels International Speedway Boulevard. There are hundreds of people in the line. The line does not move. The line only gets longer.

At the racetrack across the street Monday practice is still running wide open, and the whole blinding afternoon buzzes like a hive. Over there the line moves at 185 mph. From the pedestrian footbridge, fans leaving the track notice the sunstruck crowd surrounding the Barnes & Noble.

"Looks like Disneyland from up here, don't it?"

"Those people look baked."

"Those poor folks look like they been clubbed."

"What time's he comin'?"

"I don't know what time he starts, but I know he's gonna have a writer's cramp by the time he's done."

And at nearly that moment Dale Earnhardt Jr. ducks out of a slate-gray SUV and into the side door of the bookstore. He has come here to sign books. Many, many books.

This is February 2002. It is 51 weeks to the day, almost to the hour, since his father was killed, not quite half a mile from here, in the last turn on the last lap of the 2001 Daytona 500. It is a long time gone and he is mended now and it is safe for him to be here; or it is an excruciation, an aching, heartbreaking effort.

**TUNED IN** JUNIOR DIDN'T WANT TO BE KNOWN SIMPLY AS THE INTIMIDATOR'S SON, SO HE WENT OUT AND PROVED HE COULD DRIVE.

**PHOTOGRAPH BY GEORGE TIEDEMANN/GT IMAGES**

No one who is allowed, at last, to walk up for his swooping lasso of a signature can tell which. The weight of that name, the noise in his head, the surge and ebb in his chest are none of their business. He is unfailingly pleasant and polite with everyone.

He wears a red polo shirt and baggy khaki shorts and a red B (as in Budweiser) baseball cap clocked around aft in the trademark manner. He is pale and slender with sharp features and a quick, thin smile that seems to flicker out the moment he isn't paying attention to it. "Good to see you," he says quietly to each of them as they arrive at his table. *"Good to see you!"* they shout or shriek or sob in return, unable to modulate themselves a moment longer.

The first fan in line, Charles Long, 27, of Winter Springs, Fla., has been here since 4 a.m. because, he says, "Junior is a regular guy. Just like me. Who drinks beer. Just like me." He hoots and whoops and pumps his fists and jumps up and down when his two copies of *Driver #8* are signed. He is then overrun by a squad of beautifully groomed local television reporters.

nor unimaginably bad. Earnhardt accepts it and says, "Thank you, Buddy." Someone turns the boy around and his mother says "Smile" but he doesn't, and then the flash explodes blue and white and impossibly cold, and the two of them, man and boy, are frozen together for an instant. Forever.

WHEN I was just a little squirt, I clipped pictures of race cars from magazines and taped them to my bedroom walls. I scissored out pictures of the drivers, too, and around the room grinned the heroic faces of Hill and Clark and Stewart, the Unsers and the Pettys, Foyt, Andretti, Yarborough and Lorenzen, even the great Fangio. I dreamed of being one of them.

At night, in the desolate freedom of those dreams, I moved across a shadow landscape at terrifying speeds, goggled and tattooed with grime, an eight-year-old boy with a front-page smile, rakish and death-defying, trailing a white silk scarf and the noise of a distant crowd. Speed was everything.

## Dale Jr. is arguably the sport's first crossover star, a full-bore billboard MTV breakout bad boy, running wide-effing-open down Madison Avenue.

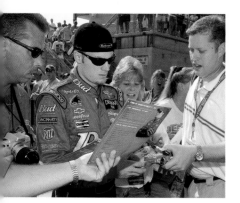

**STAR ATTRACTION** ON OR OFF THE TRACK, EARNHARDT (HERE, WITH FANS AFTER QUALIFYING FOR THE BRICKYARD 400 AT INDY IN '02) IS A CROWD-PLEASER.

For hours the others will shuffle forward, the mother and daughter teams in from Ohio, the glowering bachelors out of Tennessee, entire tomato-red families down from Jersey. Silent 60-year-old shirtless fat men in straw hats and coveralls, quivering 14-year-old girls blow-molded into their black spandex crop tops, husbands and wives in matching pictographic Dale Jr. T-shirts—everyone has a copy of the book, two copies, three, nine, to be signed. "No other merchandise," shout the book people, "will be signed!" Cameras flash, teenage girls flirt or stare or tremble in their weeping, cops roll their eyes, the line inches forward, people scale the Art & Architecture shelves for a better look. "Junior!" they shout, "Hey, Junior!" until one no-longer-young woman climbs the wedding planners display to croon, "Helloooooooo, Sexy!" and everybody breaks up. The thin smile flickers. This is how the book about #8 made it to #4 on *The New York Times* best-seller list.

A mother guides her son toward the table. He is a little boy, maybe nine, 10 years old. "Hey, Buddy," says Dale, Jr., softly. The boy doesn't say anything, nor does he have a book, and he freezes for a second, unsure what to do. His mother nudges him gently from behind. "Go ahead," she says. Expressionless, the boy hands Dale Jr. a picture he's drawn. It is a smudged pencil rendering of Earnhardt's number 8 Budweiser car, complete with cartoon speed lines trailing off the roof and rear spoiler. It is neither precociously good

Only much later did I learn that at this speed the wall is liquid. At this speed you are deaf to everything but the greedy furnace blast of the engine, blind to anything but the tunnel you drill through the glare. At this speed time itself thins and cracks into useless theory. Your future shimmers out there in that demon heat six inches ahead of you. Drive fast enough and you hit life's escape velocity: dead or famous, and you're better off either way. So manage your fear, ride it, man, keep that oily churn in your gut buckled down tight. 'Cause if you don't, it might climb into your throat and choke you.

At this speed the track swims and unspools beneath you in a murderous blur. You are fast. Fast out of all proportion to sense or physics or the slow and tortured turning of the earth, you are centrifugal, orbital, as vast and ancient and celestial as something flung down from heaven to wreak a black and unblinking havoc on a thousand thousand generations of sinners. At this speed you are the very sword of God.

At this speed you'll start Sunday's race 35th in a field of 43 cars. Or so it seems on any NASCAR qualifying day.

AT 27 Dale Earnhardt Jr., (Little E), currently embodies, metaphorically and otherwise, NASCAR's gleaming future. He is arguably the sport's first crossover star, a full-bore billboard MTV breakout bad boy (That hat! Those glasses! Rage rock! Hip-hop! Lock up your daughters, America!), running wide-effing-open down Madison Avenue, bringing beer and sass and sex into your living room.

In years past the model for the great motoring heroes of the circuit was perhaps a little, um, straight-arrow. Scrubbed a bit too clean, bled out, colorless. The Other Other White Meat. In some cases there was a bit too much red, maybe, right around the neck bone.

The muttonchops and nylon windbreakers don't peg the tach with those Greenwich focus groups. Preaching only to the converted, they sold motor oil, brake rotors and mentholated dippin' snuff.

Until the time of his father's death, Dale Jr., and to a lesser extent his brother, Kerry, a successful Busch series driver, had inspired in fans only the kind of tentative, speculative affection that surrounds the son of any famous man. Sure, he'd won two championships in the Busch series, NASCAR's Triple A circuit, but did he have the grit, the steel to run in the Show, the Winston Cup? He could drive, O.K., but the talk in the pits was that he had more *cojones* than cortex, and when was he gonna step, as they say, *Up*? Lordy, even Frank Sinatra Jr. can carry a tune. The only question is, how far?

Flung far and fast into the naked limelight by that slow-motion crash up the mountainous reach of Turn 4, Earnhardt Jr. might have become nothing more than a curiosity, another lounge act. Worse still, he might have believed all those newspapers trimmed in mourning black that presented him, generously but wrongly, as JFK Jr.: a handsome, harmless attendant of the family's eternal flame, whose public life must be lived in the long, chilly shadow of his father and whose accomplishments can't help but seem small when seen in the wan, reflected light that infrequently falls on them.

So Dale Earnhardt Jr., grandson of short track legend Ralph Earnhardt and son of the mighty Intimidator, ol' Ironhead hisself, goes out and does the onliest thing he knows to trump the lame, melodramatic script that everyone else is trying to write for him. He races. He runs, as they say, good. Top 10. Top five. He wins. At Daytona in July. At Dover. At Talladega. He finishes 2001 eighth in points and with more than $5 million in winnings. On top of that he makes monster endorsement money, and the fans' affections, their swarming passions, untethered after his father's accident, are beginning now to bear down on him.

Which brings us back to the Day of the Locust crowds that attend his every move. It starts during those two long weeks in Daytona, 2002. The book's a hit. He's everywhere on television. He can't walk anywhere without being pestered, pictured, pursued. If he stops long enough to take a breath, a bouquet of microphones materializes in front of him. He has to hide in the garage or strap himself into his car. He runs good the first few weeks. Top 10. Top five. During any given race he has more women sitting on his toolbox in the pits than most other drivers, a sure sign of, well, something. At Texas in early April he spins and wads the car up pretty good in Turn 2, and security tries to close the garage because so many fans come pouring over the fences to watch his crew try to bang the frame straight. His failures now attract greater attention than some drivers get in Victory Lane.

**THIS BUD'S FOR YOU**
SINCE HIS FATHER'S DEATH, DALE JR. (HERE QUALIFYING FOR THE '02 SIRIUS 400 IN MICHIGAN) HAS BEEN A DRIVER ON A MISSION.

At Bristol, in the surprising early-season cold of the Tennessee hills, he shows up in his pit thuggin' it, dressed like P. Diddy at Gstaad, with a knit cap pulled down to his evil shades and a mustard ski jacket the size of a spinnaker. The crowd of 147,000 pours ovations down on him in that tiny, tidy bowl. The loudest of the day comes right after the race, however, when he and Robby Gordon bang each other hard going back into pit road. It is intentional and juvenile, and it will cost them both thousands of dollars in fines. But it is also old school, Friday-night, dirt-track turf-war gamesmanship. The people roar for it, for him. In the motoring press a week later are the recriminatory editorials about sophomoric behavior and dark murmurs about a missed promotional appearance. Drowned out by the cheering, they go unheeded.

At Talladega back in April, under that angry Alabama sun, the fans rose in the stands every time Dale Jr. ran his car out for practice. In the shade of the garage between sessions he would peel himself out of the top of his driver's suit, hitch his pants and stand, flushed and frail-seeming, in front of the swamp cooler by the car. Cries of "Junior!" rang out during the prayer before the race, a 40-year-old echo of the days when Junior Johnson was the Last American Hero. When the race began, so did the roaring, from a grandstand nearly a mile long, louder even than the cars. Every time he ran out front the roar grew and people stood and people fainted in the heat and the roar swelled again and became a solid wall of noise for the last few laps and the people swooned in the light and the noise and the hot, heroic love of something they felt was bigger than all of them. And he won. At the moment he crossed the finish line, borne forward by the apocalyptic cry of 200,000 fans, scores of thousands of cameras flashed, impossibly cold and blue, the moment frozen.

WHY IS NASCAR so successful? In part because, unlike most other sports, in which fans can see only dim reflections of themselves—when was the last time you hit a 450-foot home run off a 98-mile-an-hour fastball, or carded a 63 at Medinah—NASCAR is at once death-defying and prosaic. When was the last time you drove?

NASCAR works overtime to engage its fans in many ways. Foremost among these, obviously, is the racing itself, with its manufacturer rivalries, its life-or-death risks and rewards and its stars trading paint and sharp words at speed on the high-banked ovals at Darlington or Martinsville.

NASCAR is also one of the strictest, albeit one of the most fluid, rule-making bodies in sport. The organization's nabobs intend for mechanical parity to ensure close racing and further fan interest, so they not only micromanage the engineering of the race cars at every point but also often modify the construction rules from week to week or even day to day, half an inch here, half a pound there, to prevent one make or model from gaining an unfair advantage over the others. The teams, of course, do everything they can to gain that unfair advantage, so the tension between enforcement and violation of the many technical restrictions creates a kind of nervous equilibrium. Outright cheating is now rare, but elaborate conspiracy theories still fuel the garage rumor mill.

And NASCAR, unlike sports without a central governing authority, makes sure fans have unprecedented access to the athletes—that family autograph opportunities are plentiful at every racetrack and at the many personal appearances the drivers routinely make. Like the music business down in Nashville with its annual FanFest,

**DAY AT THE OFFICE**
FOR A DRIVER, BAD CRASHES—AND EARNHARDT'S DUSTUP AT FONTANA IN '02 (ABOVE) WAS BAD—GO WITH THE TERRITORY, AS DO CELEBRATIONS (LEFT, AT TALLADEGA IN '02), SPLIT-SECOND PIT STOPS (BELOW, AT LOUDON IN '03) AND ADORING THRONGS.

NASCAR enforces a grassroots interaction between its stars and the paying customers. At a time when NFL players are nothing more to most autograph seekers than an angry silhouette behind the tinted glass of a giant SUV fleeing the stadium parking lot, NASCAR understands the responsibilities of mythmaking and corporate endorsement and touts its heroes as good ol' boys from right next door who will sign just about anything you hand them and would love to hunker down with a bottle of Bud and some nachos if they only had the time.

In the interest of customizing this mythmaking, NASCAR manufactures matinee idols of several stripes, from the young, square-jawed All-America hotshots like Jeff Gordon and Jimmie Johnson and Tony Stewart to the avuncular elders like Dale Jarrett, Mark Martin and Rusty Wallace. And once a driver earns himself a regular ride in the Show, he'll find that he's got a prefab, presold fan base and a gleaming merchandise hauler on the racetrack midway hawking his now-heroic head shot on hats and shirts and jackets.

All this is far more than a Deep South cult of personality, however. NASCAR has, for its fans from Manhattan to Manhattan Beach, transcended its self-limiting Southern origins. It has insti-

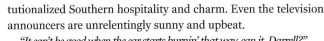

The car slides down onto the grass, vomiting steam, smoke and oil, and sits ominously. This is by far **the worst hit of his career.**

tutionalized Southern hospitality and charm. Even the television announcers are unrelentingly sunny and upbeat.

*"It can't be good when the car starts burnin' that way, can it, Darrell?"*

*"No, sir, not even one little bit!"*

Fans are also taught to cheer the teams and car owners for whom their idols race and to follow even the performance of their pit crews with an abiding passion. And, as in no other sport, fans applaud the equipment, too, devoting themselves, sometimes for life, to the cars, either Ford or Chevy, Pontiac or Dodge, driving one brand to the exclusion of all others, a loyalty manufacturers have been exploiting since stock car racing began in earnest after World War II. "Win on Sunday, sell on Monday" is as true now as it was when the hottest ride on the track was a Hudson Hornet.

In April 2002 about 100,000 fans washed over Fontana, Calif., over the track and the stands and the garages, lapping gently against the fences and the walls and the cars and the drivers. On a Saturday afternoon Dale Earnhardt Jr. watches this tide flow around him from the upholstered anonymity of his immense motor home.

Even stretched to full length on the sofa, watching yet another race on TV with his buds, he seems restless and animated, ready for something—the race tomorrow, maybe. He looks you straight in the eye when he listens and when he speaks. He can dial the North Carolina in his voice up or down, but it's nothing you could dip a biscuit in. He looks stronger, more substantial, away from the car. He is handsome, certainly, but he is not the looming Apollo his

billboards portray. He looks more like the lube 'n' tune guy he used to be at Dale Earnhardt Chevrolet than the object of national obsession he's become. In the right light he looks like a guy who looks just like the guy on the billboard.

"Two years ago, when I'd walk from my motor coach to the car in practice, there were less than half the people asking for autographs, so I see that there's a big change as far as the hard-core fans that we have now. It's changed quite a bit. There's a responsibility that goes with it now. A lot of the fans say, 'Man, we like you because you're yourself—stay yourself, always be yourself.' And that's true to a point, but I'm finding now, more and more, that we're under the microscope, that some of the things I would do in the past aren't accepted now. Something that was just a prick on the rosebush before is a huge problem now, something I might say in an interview or something. It's taken quite a lot more seriously now." And he's

## "I used to miss him every minute," Dale Jr. says about his father. "Now I've got it down to about every five minutes."

right. His every remark is broadcast, typeset, satellited, sent resonating down that clacking NASCAR telegraph.

On his way out the door for yet another interview he is confronted by thousands of reminders of his father—portraits, banners, flags snapping in the breeze. "I used to miss him every minute," he says. "Now I've got it down to about every five minutes." Then he's gone.

On the 228th lap at Fontana, Kevin Harvick cuts a tire coming through Turn 4 and swerves dead left into the right rear quarter panel of the devil-red number 8. Betrayed by a sudden absence of traction and Sir Isaac Newton's buzz-killer humbug on the subjects of mass and force and momentum, Dale Earnhardt Jr. is launched uphill into the wall. Spinning, he hits first front then rear, hard; hard enough to accordion the car down to about two thirds of its original length; hard enough to bring an audible gasp from the frontstretch grandstand; hard enough even to silence the TV announcers, if only briefly. The car slides down onto the grass, vomiting steam and smoke and oil, and sits ominously, heavily there for what seems like a long time. This is by far the worst hit of his career. In less than 30 seconds, though, the EMTs have him out of the car. Bent double, grimacing, he has had the wind knocked out of him.

Twenty minutes later he comes swinging out the doors of the infield medical center on crutches. He sprained an ankle when he braced his feet against the fire wall. Torqued a shoulder joint, too, and the russet bloom of his bruises is just beginning. Nothing serious. He is pissed off and joking, but mostly pissed off, and his one grumbled comment, "I hit hard, goddammit, you know the rest," will no doubt have to be translated into uplifting, PG-rated sports jabber for the morning papers.

Fans throng the fence line as Earnhardt is driven away on a golf

cart, applauding, whistling, bellowing encouragement. One man, though, remains still. He is a round little handful of a man, maybe 40 or so, and he holds above the fence, at stubby arm's length, a large mirror framed in rococo gilt. It's the kind of thing you'd see in a sports bar or an overdone rumpus room. Across its bright face in lurid Victorian gold and red stencil it reads BUDWEISER CONGRATULATES DALE EARNHARDT JR. He holds it as high as he can, dazzling in the sun, until Junior is gone. Before anyone can ask why he's brought it here, he, too, slips away. Whatever did he expect Dale Earnhardt Jr., or any one of us, to see in it?

FROM A sport whose origins are rooted in the misty hills and hollers of the postwar rural South, where the white-lightning ridge runners boomed through the moonless night trying to outrun the po-leece and the gubmint revenuers, NASCAR has evolved into the new model for the synergies of cutting-edge, multiplatform, cross-promotional corporate performance. And Dale Earnhardt Jr., whose fame is now self-sustaining and whose career arc will become the responsibility largely of strangers, who is the Next

American Hero or the new Eddie Haskell, depending on who does the telling, will be asked, like it or not, to carry it all forward on his perfectly average, 40-regular shoulders.

At Richmond, the first weekend of May, he crashes unremarkably and limps out of that rain-swollen weekend 12th in points for the season. Two weeks later he electrifies the crowd at Charlotte with a late-night, last-lap charge to the front in the Winston, NASCAR's cannily formatted All-Star street fight. By choosing not to punt eventual winner Ryan Newman out of his way with two turns left in the race, Earnhardt Jr. forfeits around $750K but earns the manic affection of the motoring press and several hundred 24-karat column inches on the topics of probity, maturity and good sportsmanship. "Getting to him was easy," says Junior at the media center just before midnight, "getting by him was something different."

A week later he runs well until he gets tangled up with a slower car and brushes the wall. The car goes sour; then it overheats and goes away entirely, and he finishes deep in the field at the Coca-Cola 600. At Dover, Del., he finishes 30th and drops to 14th in the points race. At Pocono he's 12th. At Michigan, 22nd. At Sonoma, 30th.

**THE TEAM** DALE JR. (HERE, WITH DALE SR. AT DAYTONA DURING SPEED WEEKS 2001) HAS FELT THE WEIGHT OF INCREASED FAN EXPECTATIONS OVER THE PAST TWO YEARS.

Everywhere they scream for him as the season inches on.

His future, whatever it may be, will draft a survey of the entire NASCAR landscape, across which roll and intersect not only the easy streams of popular culture, in which we find the commonplace objects of our desire—cars and money and fame— but also the wide, hard ribbons of American religion and race and class. NASCAR distills to an essence America's obsession with speed and sex and death. In it beats the heart of our national experience as citizen consumers and hellbent rebel yellers. In it lies our central postmodern metaphor: racing ever faster in circles, chasing a buck. In it we fire and forge our next generation of American Heroes. In it we rediscover our restless frontier habits, our deep rural need to move fast across the land, fleeing the oppression of boredom, pursuing a different sun gone down on a new horizon and finding at the end of that day peace or satisfaction or perhaps only, ever, always, ourselves.  □

His future, whatever it may be, **will draft a survey of the entire NASCAR landscape,** across which roll the easy streams of popular culture and the wide, hard ribbons of American religion and race and class.

**THE ONE** WHEN DALE JR. DRIVES (HERE, AT RICHMOND IN '01), IT'S NO EXAGGERATION TO SAY THAT NASCAR NATION TAGS ALONG FOR THE RIDE.

# LAST LAP

Fans at the Aaron's 499 at Talladega last April **showed their colors** as eventual winner Dale Earnhardt Jr. and the rest of the pack roared past the grandstand.

**PHOTOGRAPH BY JONATHAN FERREY/GETTY IMAGES**